HANG 'EM

...on their history

Donald E. Crosley

Montana Vigilante Crusade 1860's

Printed in the United States of America

First Printing, 2013

ISBN 978-1-4675-9214-7

Cover Illustration and Design, Amanda M. Morton

Insty Prints
120 West Park Street
Butte, Montana 59701

www.instybutte.com

Table of Contents

ILLUSTRATIONS and PHOTOGRAPHS

ACKNOWLEDGMENTS

Special thanks to the following people:

Family and friends for their encouragement and support over the past years.

Chris Fisk and Jeanette Larson for their reviews of the book and encouragement.

Rose Sladek and Insty-Prints for their suggestions and excellent work in helping get this book published.

Amanda Morton for her patience and hard work on the book design and for the wonderful sketches.

Last, but not least, to my wife of 49 years, Patricia, for her support, patience, editing and help to get my book finished and finally published.

Don Crosley

INTRODUCTION

The history of the Montana Vigilantes begins with the cause for their formation, the intrusion of the "ne'er-do-well" into a society of hard working gold seekers in the growing Northwest Territories.

The lure of gold brought seekers of wealth from across the seas, onto the lands of America, and then West across sparsely populated mountains and plains. With those who sought wealth and were willing to work for it, came the criminal faction...those who would connive ways to reap the fruit of labor...without the labor! One such young man, Henry Plumer, sailed from Maine to San Francisco. He was energetic, beguiling and entrepreneurial. After his trials and tribulations, which included a killing and time spent in San Quentin prison in California, his name mistakenly became "Plummer." After several jousts with the law, both as a defender and a spoiler, Plummer's experiences left him longing for home.

However, he missed his boat home in the lonely Northwest, but met a young maiden at a newly established government farm. Love delayed Plummer's everlasting lust for wealth...but only shortly...its growing lure took him into the rich gold country.

On the steamship in San Francisco Bay, a passenger with Plummer, a former banker and supplier of mining equipment, would lead a questionable group to the newest gold strike at a lonesome town in the Northwest called Bannack.

A group of ne'er-do-wells followed an entrepreneurial merchant from Elk City into Bannack. The merchant sold his goods for a large amount of gold. He was offered "security" for the balance of his return trip home by the same nefarious group. They were interested more in the wealth gained from his sales, than his safe trip home.

The onset of ruthless criminal activity in the gold rich area had become overpowering without law or form of deterrence. Outraged citizens banded to form a group, not to formulate laws, but to fight to enforce their survival. Their new group grew, as adversaries plundered, until they became feared, even by those they protected. Their members grew...in numbers and power...and became known as vigilantes...the *Montana Vigilantes!*

They became "ruthless" in their justice. Death!...by hanging! Their *Justice* created fear in the hearts of belligerent robbers and killers...those still alive!

The *Vigilantes* had a job forced upon them and they survived...into history!

FOREWORD
HANG 'EM...ON THEIR HISTORY

Gold was found in the Southwest corner of what is now Montana... far from anywhere and everyone. Rich gold strikes in the Rocky Mountains turned small nondescript areas into bustling towns. The gold was found to be of the highest and richest grade anywhere in the country. The word was out..."Gold"...and the stampede began!

These new strikes in the far north, would draw high interest from the hungry miners of the Gold Rush in California. They flocked north to the small but growing town of Bannack in the Southeastern corner of Washington Territory (Idaho and Montana). Seeking the richest rewards, many honest, hard working, gold-diggers migrated north into the Rocky Mountains, followed by scavengers and unscrupulous fortune hunters.

A young man from the Eastern coast of Maine, as many others, followed the lure of gold and sailed to California. Only nineteen years old, the young adventurer landed at San Francisco in May of 1852. He worked his way east, and over time to Nevada City, where an opening in the Sheriff's office brought him the job of Marshal. He errantly killed a man, over a woman, and was sentenced to ten years at San Quentin prison. He concocted a ploy against the warden, served less than six months and was pardoned in 1859. He returned to Nevada City in California. His family name was misspelled in prison and soon he became known as Plummer...Henry Plummer!

The gold bug took young Plummer into the eastern portion of Washington Territory, soon to become the Territories of Idaho and Montana. As a gambler he played his cards right, except those under the table, and soon became Sheriff in the rich and booming gold town of Bannack (Montana).

The name Henry Plummer became synonymous with robberies and killing from Bannack to the newest gold strike in the area...Virginia City. Plummer's lucrative robberies continued until the citizenry rose up and formed a vigilante group to combat his crime...soon to become the "Montana Vigilantes!"

This group of miners, shopkeepers, ranchers and lawyers...put a noose in the face of crime. Their actions were described by some in history as "ruthless"...even criminal. Even without written law, they got the job done...the Vigilantes were the judge...the jury...the court and the executioner. The 1860's of Montana's history was bloody...with many heroic and outstanding "Players."

Henry Plummer had entered into the history of the 1860's and become, just that ...history. Others would come to test the will of the Vigilantes. One such harbinger of ill will would be a hard worker of the Overland Freight lines...Jack Slade. He was a leader of stage-hands and tough at his job. His personality would lead to his confrontation with Vigilante Law.

As leader, Slade controlled his men with brute force, even to the shooting of some of his stage-hands. His destructive policy of punishment, such as the hanging of errant workers, became known, but not confronted. After he retired from Overland and lived in Virginia City, his drunken attitude brought him to confront James Williams, a strong willed leader of the Vigilantes. Williams warned Slade his boisterous actions of threatening a Judge with a pistol could not be tolerated...he had to pay!

The Montana Vigilantes continued to enforce their form of law and order. In March of 1864, Montana Territory was established with laws and enforcement. The original Vigilantes had become the major protector against criminal behavior. They were ordered to quit by Chief Justice Hosmer...and they did...twice. However, a new group of "Copycat" Vigilantes formed and continued hanging rustlers in the cattle country of the Montana plains until the 1880's. Nathanial P. Langford was important in the foundation of Montana's famous, or infamous history...because he was a major "Player" of that history...a witness to many of the events he later wrote about. Many historical writers, used in reference, have added to the verification, additional insight, or shown knowledge and skill interpreting the facts, events and personalities of 150 years past.

Langford, with astute knowledge of the English language, rewrote "quotes" of other Players in his book, *"Vigilante Days and Ways,"* into "proper" verbiage. They are perceived to be correct. However, their true distinction, or meaning of what may have been actually spoken...is somewhat lost. Langford's "quotes" are his interpretation.

Some writers, following Langford, have rewritten his quotes for modern day emphasis, but most have not. Any obscure items or facts in Langford's book, or writings of other authors used in reference, have been verified and clarification added...if needed...but not changed.

In September of 1863, Sidney Edgerton, with Colonel Wilbur F. Sanders, came west to the Territories. Edgerton would later be appointed Governor of the new Territory of Montana. Sanders, a lawyer, became well known as Prosecutor of George Ives for murder in Nevada City... Montana...its first trial.

The author's visualization of Colonel Sanders serving history as the backbone, or "Ramrod," of the Vigilante hierarchy can be subject to scrutiny.

Thomas Dimsdale, editor of the *"Montana Post"* in Virginia City, protected Vigilante Players by using numbers in his newspaper, instead of their names. Many of the Vigilantes were also members of the Masonic Lodge, whose culture of the time may have hidden many Vigilante actions, as well as some of the real heroes of this Vigilante era. Many more facts and truths, or untruths, of Montana history may yet be revealed, only time will tell...all the evidence is not yet in.

As Nathanial P. Langford wrote to his friend, Francis M. Thompson, following their historic time in Montana, *"I am very glad that you are putting your pioneer experiences in form of preservation, for every item of our early history that can be rescued from oblivion is so much gained to all who may come after us."* Langford authored historically renowned, *"Vigilante Days and Ways"* (1890) and Thompson wrote his equally renowned, *"A Tenderfoot in Montana"*...both are truly acknowledged as "Players" in the formation of the history of Montana. Plummer had entered into history of the 1860's and became just that... history! That history, not to be forgotten, or misinterpreted, must be retold!

D Crosley...4/2012

Early day photographs of Bannack, Montana, heart of the 1860's Gold Country of Montana.

Photographs courtesy of Gordon "Tex" Marchesseault, Polaris, Montana.

CHAPTER 1
HENRY PLUMMER comes to MONTANA
1852 to 1857, Fall, 1862

MOVING IN...to Montana

In early September 1862, Henry Plummer and companion Charles Reeves rode into Idaho Territory headed for the new gold strike on Grasshopper Creek at Bannack. With the luster of the Idaho gold fields at Lewiston being played out, Plummer and Reeves sought more rewarding opportunities. They rode across the Clearwater and the Bitterroot Mountains and through the mile-high Lolo Pass. Close to the small settlement of Hell Gate they met a pair of riders, Granville Stuart and Frank Woody.

Stuart had just been elected County Commissioner for the new Missoula County in the large northwest Washington Territory, where his brother, James Stuart, had been elected Sheriff. Granville Stuart was headed to Hell Gate to set up County administration offices and asked them to ride along with him. Plummer and Reeves agreed and stayed in Gold Creek for several days. Both Stuart and Woody were cautious toward Plummer and his friend, but finally formed a limited trust for them. James Stuart helped repair the broken stock on Plummer's shotgun. Plummer was unaware the Stuart brothers, just months earlier, had participated in the first hanging in the new Idaho Territory! [1]

The questionable history of Henry Plummer does not begin in Montana, but it would end there. The formation of citizens was necessary to curb the lust of Plummer and the whirlwind of robberies and crime brought on by this errant seeker of wealth. The echo of this killer still haunts Montana citizens 150 years hence. New information, letters, documents and diaries yet to turn up, may still reveal additional light on how the upcoming formation of relentless guardians would thwart Plummer and his cohorts.

These "guardians" would live, work and die in the area and would play a major role as the *Vigilantes of Montana!* Western and Montana history is yet to be written!

HISTORY...Nebulous...at best

A brief look into Plummer's prior history in California and the Idaho Territory may provide further insight into how and why he came to Montana. *(See Addendum - Players' Portraits -Plummer)*.

Earlier, in the winter of 1846-47 a group of pioneers forged new lives in the west, particularly California. Led by brothers, George and Jacob Donner from Springfield, Illinois, they joined a larger wagon train, also headed west. They soon decided to split from the larger train and take a "shortcut" across the rugged Sierra-Nevada mountains into California. The Donner Party gathered in Reno to rest as intense storms brewed in the mountains of Northern California. In their attempt to cross the rugged mountains, the snowstorms, starvation and freezing temperatures, forced them into cannibalism to survive. Only forty-seven of the group reached California, forty-two died. Less than two years later the great California Gold Rush enhanced, for those who survived, the hope of a better life. Gold became the entity for success of that nebulous hope.

Early in 1853, Henry Plummer had saved some money and took a turn at ranching. With a partner he raised cattle north of a small gold rush town, Nevada City, California, about 150 miles northeast of San Francisco. His enthusiasm for ranching lasted less than a year. Moving into Nevada City, the bustling mining town with the third largest population in California, he became a salesman for a local bakery. At twenty-one, he liked the hustle of urban life, the people, the saloons...and the company of women. He progressed as salesman, earning enough to buy out one partner's share of the United States Bakery. He also bought a small two-room bungalow on Spring Street, his first own home. His idea to sell the bakery and reopen at a new location proved to be a financial disaster. The economy was down and Plummer was ready to quit the West and go home, but he changed his mind.

As luck would have it, a vacancy opened in the Sheriff's office and the city council hired Plummer as a deputy. Six months later in a close election, Plummer defeated his chief and became the Marshal of Nevada City. Plummer's new position cast him into the hotbed of California politics. [2]

A new political movement was growing across the country..."The Know-Nothings." The threat of job security for the native-born workers in the East was fueled by the rush of immigrants from across the Atlantic. In northern California the Know-Nothing movement formed to deal with a similar migration to the West by the Chinese. The movement's secrecy among the early members, the use of special signs, passwords, handshakes, and the "I know nothing" answer, if questioned about their activities, must have been of some interest to Plummer...but he joined the Democratic Party instead. The Know-Nothing secrecy to protect member identities, the use of signs and passwords, would stay in Plummer's mind, and become part of his future gang of nefarious robbers and killers. [3]

EDUCATION...by experience

Henry Plummer, only twenty-four years old, now had a position serving the public of Nevada City, requiring a depth of knowledge and competence, from keeping pigs off the streets to corralling drunken killers. It also took knowledge of when not to interfere. Earlier, on June 6, 1856, a Friday night with only a month on the job, Plummer gained some costly experience.

On a casual night out, Plummer and two friends, entered a bar. A shoving match between a couple of drunken customers erupted. The bar was rocked and glasses were broken. Plummer intervened and attempted to arrest the men. The bar-owner, Lewis, fervently objected and stated he would take care of his customers and didn't need the Marshal's interference. One of Plummer's friends, George Jordan, angrily interrupted Lewis, who pulled a pistol from under the bar and fired at Jordan, missing him but hitting one of the men who started the ruckus. Plummer, armed only with a nightstick could do no more than watch. Lewis fired again, hitting Jordan in the chest, killing him. The man first shot, attacked Lewis, but Plummer subdued the fight and arrested Lewis. The wounded drunk escaped...howling...into the night. The night ended with two men shot, one dead, one arrested for murder. Plummer was harshly ridiculed by the local newspaper for not *"keeping the peace and quiet of the town!"*

Plummer used this event as good experience for the future. He learned to evaluate future situations before taking action and started to carry a pistol and used it with deadly skill. He spoke in an even and firm voice which demanded attention. He would also learn to choose trustworthy companions who would not override his authority.

Jordan, who had interfered in Plummer's behalf, had been out of jail on bail, arrested for breaking a man's jaw just hours before he was shot by Lewis. Plummer's newly learned traits were frequently acknowledged by many people he would later encounter, both friend and foe. [4]

SHOOTING MATCH...by mistake

On July 19, 1856, a fire broke out in a blacksmith shop, spread and consumed half of Nevada City. In its wake it destroyed the new courthouse, a part of the jail, killing ten people. The fire and the previous bar episode proved to widen the existing rift between Sheriff Wright and Marshal Plummer. Sheriff Wright hired a deputy, David Johnson, who had earlier been defeated by Plummer in the election for Marshal. Many in the County were disgruntled, including Plummer, who proclaimed Sheriff

19

Wright had more authority in law enforcement than he did.

Meanwhile, robber Jim Webster, arrested earlier by Plummer, escaped from the damaged jail. Plummer tracked him down, jailed him again...and he escaped again! He fled with two other robbers, brothers named Farnsworth. Plummer had a good idea where the escapees would be hiding, but seemed in no hurry to begin the manhunt, even though he had been warned horses were ready near the suspected hiding place of the escapees.

Plummer planned to use only one deputy to pursue and capture the fugitives. His delay tactic kept Wright from following him. However, when Plummer started out, Wright found out and quickly followed him. As Plummer approached the suspected cabin, Wright and Deputy Johnson rode up with two others. Plummer sensed another group of men nearby. One of the group shouted, *"Don't come any closer!"* Before Plummer could answer, Johnson yelled back, *"What are you doing here?"*

Seconds later multiple shots rang out. Plummer realized the shots came from a group of Vigilantes, who had feared he would not do his job...and decided to do it for him. Plummer recognized someone in the flash of gunfire and shouted, *"Stop firing! You're killing your friends!"*

The shooting stopped, but Sheriff Wright lay dead of multiple wounds. David Johnson, mortally wounded, was taken to a nearby home of one of the Vigilantes. In Plummer's recorded account of the shooting, he concluded, "...we knew it was a mistake." The coroner's verdict... *"Accidental death."* Plummer was vindicated, but Editor of the local *Journal*, Wallace Williams, apparently a supporter if not a member of the Vigilantes, was not content. He claimed Plummer was a coward and reported in the newspaper, *"I suppose Plummer took to his heels and ran after he fired."*

On November 19, 1856, Plummer, infuriated, wrote a letter to the *Nevada Democrat*, *"I would gladly forget all the deplorable events of that tragedy, but I cannot permit the sneering insinuations to go unnoticed."* He concluded, *"I will leave this subject with the hope that he (Williams) may enjoy the reputation for which he longs and I, such as I deserve."* Williams accused Plummer of acting like a *"...spoiled child!"*

Again, the lack of diplomacy between the Sheriff's office and that of the Marshal left two men dead, several wounded and three robbers still on the loose. The escaped prisoners, the major point of the escapade, were never caught.

Although Plummer's reputation and ego were marred, he recovered and restored both. He hunted down and captured fugitives until he regained public approval.

In May of 1857, Plummer was reelected Marshal. Three months later, at the County Democratic convention, Plummer was one of five men nominated as candidates to the Lower House of the California Legislature. However, accusations of Plummer, mixed with the unsavory faction of saloons and brothels, took root with a group of miners who previously favored him and he was defeated. His political aspirations doomed, Plummer continued to serve the Nevada City public as Marshal. [5]

FRISCO POLITICS...cronies ousted

Meanwhile back in California, following two shootings which left a federal Marshal and a prominent newspaper editor dead, the San Francisco Committee of Vigilance, with a membership of some six thousand, was revived. On May 22, 1856, led by a millionaire contractor and a veteran of the 1851 Vigilantes, the new San Francisco Vigilantes seized Charles Cora and James Casey. They were taken from the jail and lynched in full public view. Cora killed a federal marshal at an opera house for belittling his girlfriend. Casey shot and killed a newspaper publisher for printing his past prison record at Sing-Sing prison. Shortly afterwards, two other men were also executed by the Vigilantes. Dozens of corrupt politicos were driven into exile including David Broderick, a devious political leader. The Vigilante members then took charge of City Hall and cleaned out more political cronies.

The San Francisco Vigilantes were highly repulsed by the lack of justice they had seen. They acted and were widely applauded. The wide public approval of the Vigilante revival affected politicians from the Governor's mansion down to the Nevada City office of Marshal Plummer. Plummer formed a distrust of such type of "peoples " justice, taking utter contempt for "Vigilante Law" as a threat against his personal safety. [6]

Chapter Notes

Note 1. The history of Henry Plummer, or "Plumer," is nebulous. There are many versions by the multitude of writers on the subject. Genealogical data shows more than one "Henry" in the census records of Maine in the 1860's, the time frame used to trace him. One family from Maine headed west to Wisconsin, but there was no trace farther west. The family of Moses and Abigail Plumer, with three siblings to "Henry," is deemed most probable. There is controversy among writers regarding N.P. Langford and E. Purple's later meeting with the remaining sister and brother of Henry in New York.

Note 2. Newly formed Missoula County was still part of the Washington Territory as was most of the western part of present day Montana. "Montana" as noted, once part of the Washington Territory becomes Idaho Territory (1863). In May 1864, a bill for a new territory was approved by Congress. President Lincoln signed it establishing the Montana Territory.

Note 3. "Nevada City"...California or Montana? Henry Plummer visited both in his lifetime. This Chapter takes place in California, in the mountains bordering the state of Nevada, between Reno and Sacramento. Plummer doesn't visit Nevada City (Montana) until November, 1862. (see Chapter 4.)

CHAPTER 2
PLUMMER'S PLOY in SAN QUENTIN
Spring, 1857 to Fall, 1859

PLUMMER LOVES...and kills

In the spring of 1857, Lucinda and husband John Vedder rented an apartment on Spring Street in Nevada City (California) from Henry Plummer. They had a three-year-old daughter and after several years of a distraught marriage were on the verge of divorce. Both had quick tempers. Lucy questioned John about spying on her. John responded by threatening her with a Bowie knife to her throat. The next day she contacted Marshal Plummer and asked him for help. He recommended a mutually known lawyer, David Belden, to offer legal advice. John Vedder met with Belden, but showed anger when asked who was intervening in his marital affairs. John Vedder suspected Plummer. Belden felt Vedder's anger and refused to talk with him.

Lucy and her daughter moved into a room at the Hotel de Paris. She still went back to the rented home on Spring Street to fix meals for her husband. Plummer, seemingly concerned about Lucy's safety, rented an apartment in the hotel across the hall from her. This aroused concern not only with her husband, but with the townspeople. Plummer asked Pat Corbett, a former deputy, to stay with him in the room as chaperone. But people talked and Vedder's anger grew. He took his young daughter away from Lucy, back to his home.

He later told friends he meant to kill Plummer for having an affair with his wife. He brandished a knife, saying he preferred it over a pistol. Plummer told several people John has had a "hard lot," and could face kidnaping charges. Plummer would hold a vigil eye on Vedder's actions.

John Vedder contacted Belden on Friday morning, September 25 and asked that divorce papers be prepared, signed and processed. Belden agreed, but noticed Vedder seemed agitated, with something else on his mind.

The day before, Vedder had taken his daughter to a ranch where he lived with Lucy before they moved to town. Vedder asked the ranch owner, Van Young, to keep and guard his daughter in case Lucy or Plummer attempted to take her. Vedder had agreed, in the signed and filed divorce papers, to surrender the child to Lucy, but it appeared that was not his intention. Friday afternoon Vedder went to the Hotel de Paris and ordered dinner, but left without eating. He arranged for the rental of a horse, then asked to borrow a pistol from a friend, who obtained a gun and gave it to him, not knowing why Vedder needed it, or what his intentions were.

Meanwhile, after her husband had left the Hotel de Paris, Lucy Vedder met with Pat Corbett at the hotel to have dinner. Both Lucy and Corbett went back to Spring Street to finish her packing. John was expected to soon deliver their daughter to Lucy, not knowing she planned to take her back to Sacramento.

Vedder had earlier checked on his daughter at Van Young's ranch and rode back to town, returning the horse to the stable. Close to midnight, he went to the rented home on Spring Street and started up the back stairs of the house, gun in hand.

VEDDER'S PLAN...shoot to kill

Shortly before midnight, Friday, September 25, 1857, Plummer arrived at Spring Street to relieve Corbett, who left. Plummer and Lucy talked and waited the arrival of John.

Suddenly, the dark silence was broken by four rapid gunshots. Neighbors reported Plummer exited the house, out the open front door, onto Spring Street and blew his police whistle. Lucy followed Plummer, crying her husband had been shot.

First on the scene was neighbor Thomas Couts. He found John Vedder lying at the bottom of the back stairs to the house. Barely alive, Vedder had been shot with a bloodstain on the left side of his white shirt. By his side, barely visible, lay a Colt revolver. Lucy returned to comfort Vedder...but he was dead! A constable, J. C. Mallory, arrived only minutes later. As neighbors gathered, Lucy told Mallory Plummer had shot her husband.

Plummer told the Constable John Vedder had climbed the back stairs to the house, stepped into the kitchen, pointed a pistol at him and shouted, *"Your time has come!"* Plummer declared he was unsure who fired first, only that he had fired several times...he thought he had surely hit Vedder.

The next day several members of the coroner's jury inspected the scene, but found no evidence Vedder had fired at Plummer. Vedder had been shot twice, in the chest and the arm. Two other pistol balls were found, one in the wall of the privy just behind the house and another in the fence at the bottom of the stairs, accounting for all four shots by Plummer.

DOCTOR'S EXAM...lots of questions

Doctors examined Vedder's wounds and determined he had been shot from above. A man sleeping in a nearby unfinished house, later testified he saw the trajectory of the shots as *"...downward."*

Both Lucy Vedder and Pat Corbett corroborated Plummer's story at the inquest, but to no avail. The Judge bound Plummer over to a Grand Jury and set bail at $8,000. On October 15, 1857, the Nevada County Grand Jury indicted Plummer for murder. The trial was set to begin December 21. On Sunday afternoon, December 27, after deliberating less than a day, the jury found Plummer guilty of second degree murder.

On Wednesday, December 30, the day set for sentencing, Belden charged three of the jurors of bias against Plummer prior to the trial and requested a new trial. The Judge denied the request and sentenced Plummer to twelve years hard labor at San Quentin prison.

BELDEN'S APPEAL...granted

On January 18, 1858, because of the bad publicity he had received, Plummer was forced to resign as Marshal. The public also claimed Plummer seduced Lucy Vedder and planned to put her into a life of prostitution and vice.[1]

However, the judge had reservations about Belden's claim of Juror bias, and granted Plummer a new trial. On September 16, 1858, the trial began in Marysville, California, a mining town 30 miles west of Nevada City.

Another appeal by Belden failed and Henry Plummer was sent to San Quentin Prison on February 22, 1859. Plummer's health was failing...but his mind was not...he would be out of prison in less than a year.

Plummer, Convict Number 1573, stood five foot eight and one half inches, weighed one hundred fifty pounds, had two moles on the back of his neck, another under his shoulder blade and bore an ugly scar on his left forefinger. Three other fingers on his left hand were permanently crippled, curled inward by scar tissue from a deep cut. The prison medical examination also disclosed Plummer's chronic lung illness...he used this illness to his favor.

PLUMMER'S PLOY...it works

Due to his frail condition the prison doctor gave him special assignment as assistant in the infirmary, let him sleep in sick bay and perform out-of-prison errands. On one such errand Plummer was caught in a coastal squall. Chilled, he became sick and awoke the next morning coughing with a fever. A blood spattered pillow led the prison doctor to diagnose Plummer as having consumption, or tuberculosis, and placed him in quarantine. On July 14, 1859, after close monitoring of Plummer's condition, a petition signed by two prison physicians was sent to Governor Weller. It stated Plummer had only five or six weeks to live and requested his release from prison. The prison doctor expressed in a personal note to Governor Weller that Plummer should be pardoned, *"... in order to die among his friends."* On August 15, 1859, Governor Weller issued the pardon, citing, *"...imminent danger of death..."* Plummer became a free man...in less than six months he was out of prison! He returned to Nevada City within a week feeling rather robust. He did not die. Fully recovered he returned to work for his friend, Marshal E.O. Tompkins, as constable on the Nevada City police force. Did he con the prison doctors with his cunning, affable attitude? Was it his blood on the pillow? There were many unanswered questions. Was this a "ploy" by Plummer to gain his freedom? Apparently it succeeded! [2] [3]

Chapter Notes

Note 1. This book involves two locations - Nevada City in California and Nevada City in Montana, both visited by Henry Plummer. This chapter refers to the California location in the mountains bordering the state of Nevada, between Reno and Sacramento. Nevada City, Montana is located in the SW corner of the state and directly north of Virginia City and mentioned in later chapters.

CHAPTER 3
EXPERIENCE - TRUE TEACHER
Spring, 1860 to Fall, 1862

MORE EXPERIENCE...all bad

In the late spring of 1860, Henry Plummer applied for and secured the position of Constable of Nevada City, California, but soon lost it when his chief is voted out of office. He decided to go east with the rush of gold seekers to Carson City, Nevada...to the new Comstock Lode. He filed several gold and silver claims, but returned to the California gold fields at Nevada City in the fall of the year. He attempted to use politics to regain his former respectability. He joined a Democratic club supporting Stephan Douglas for President. It didn't work. The townspeople of Nevada City still had a poor opinion of him. Plummer decided to return to the life he felt most comfortable in...the saloons and bordellos. He began drinking regularly and dating prostitutes.

On February 13, 1861, Plummer was with a companion at Irish Maggie's Bordello, when W. J. Muldoon banged at the door and demanded to be let into the prostitute's room. Plummer opened the door, cursed Muldoon, then struck him savagely on the head with the butt of his pistol. Muldoon staggered out of the brothel into the street dazed. He was assisted into a store and a physician was called to care for his wound. It was thought he would surely die, but he survived.

No arrest was made, but Plummer, leery of the situation, slipped out of town back to his claims on the Comstock Lode. He later returned on several occasions and openly befriended Muldoon. This proved to be a lucky move for Plummer because Muldoon took a turn for the worse and died several weeks later. Plummer was not charged with the beating or death of Muldoon.

RILEY...bad cut

Plummer stayed in Nevada City and continued to frequent the brothels. On the last Sunday in October, 1861, in the foyer of the Ashmore brothel, Plummer, who supported the Union cause, was drawn into a heated argument about the war with Southern sympathizer, William Riley. Riley lunged at Plummer with a knife, cut through his hat and sliced a deep three-inch wound along Plummer's hairline. Plummer pulled his pistol, shot and killed Riley. Plummer was quickly jailed.

A doctor closed the deep cut, but Plummer too weak to stand long, laid in his cell and worried about being sent back to prison. Allowed visitors, one of Plummer's girl friends who came to the jail claimed to be his wife. The jailers, overly relaxed, showed her into his cell. Moments later Plummer silently slipped out of his cell, into the street and disappeared. A brief, but unenthusiastic, search was conducted without results.

An editor of the *Democrat* newspaper, a one time political ally of Plummer wrote, *"If Plummer shows as much tact in staying away from the county as he did in leaving the jail, the community should have no particular reason to deplore his departure...,"* and further considered Plummer as, *"...a most useless if not a dangerous man."* Nevada City bids farewell, and good riddance, to Henry Plummer.

MAYFIELD...hideout

Plummer, still suffering from the knife wound, made his way back to Carson City and sought out Billy Mayfield, a gambler and petty criminal. Mayfield agreed to hide Plummer at his cabin. John Blackburn, the Carson City Sheriff, heard Plummer could be hiding in the area. Plummer feared the Sheriff may find him and convinced Mayfield to move him to another cabin, with a mattress and several days' food. At a meeting in a saloon on November 18, 1861, Blackburn's suspicions festered, and he attempted to arrest Mayfield. However, Mayfield resisted, pulled a knife, stabbed Blackburn several times in the chest, and killed him. Mayfield was quickly arrested and while he awaited trial for murder, Plummer quietly slipped out of town.

After leaving Carson City, Plummer's actions and location were unknown. Rumors abound, from sightings in Salt Lake City to Walla Walla, Washington. There had been a report, by a hopeful but wrong newspaper, that Plummer had been hanged.

In the Northwest, the winter of 1861-62 was the worst many could remember. It was improbable Plummer could hide anywhere in the freezing hills.

On July 24, 1862, the hotel registry of the Luna House in Lewiston, (Idaho) was signed by "Henry Plumer." (The signature was of the original family name, not as misused in history. San Quentin prison documents used both).

ORO FINO...a shoot out

Late in July, 1862, Henry Plummer, had a chance at a new life in the Lewiston gold fields. Who did he ride into the Lewiston "diggings" with?...two escapees of San Quentin prison, William Ridgley and Charles

Reeves. Plummer would spend only a short time in the Lewiston gold fields.

In August, before checking back into the Luna House, Plummer met Pat Ford, a dance hall owner, who usually followed the mining crowd, supplying miners with music, booze and girls. A friend of law and order, Ford strongly urged the elimination of drunken gangs in the gold rush area.

Ford had planned a party at Oro Fino, one of the nearby gold camps. Plummer and his two companions decided to attend the party. Again the "saloon devils" rose up in Plummer and all three men got drunk and started rough-housing. Ford, aware of possible trouble, ordered Plummer and his friends to leave, but not liking orders, a fracas broke out between Plummer and Ford. Tables were overturned, glasses and drinks were thrown about, even a pet dog of one of the women guests had its tail cut off in the drunken melee. Plummer and gang realized their company was not appreciated and decided they better leave. They started for the corral to get their horses. Ford overbearingly pushed them out the door...and the shooting began. Ridgley, was shot twice in the leg, another shot killed Plummer's horse. Plummer and his friends returned fire...killing Ford! Irate friends and customers of Ford rallied to lynch the Plummer trio, forcing them to flee the area.

Plummer caught and rode Ford's horse, but Ridgley, wounded and unable to ride, was hidden at a nearby ranch. Plummer and Reeves rode out of town and luckily escaped the lynch-mad mob.

Billy Mayfield, who had earlier killed Sheriff Blackburn, and hid Plummer, escaped prison and resurfaced in Idaho. He led a drunken gang-raid in nearby Florence, shot up the town, plundered hotels, stores and bars. Because of his earlier alliance with Mayfield, Plummer was thought to be part of the drunken raid. He was not, but it made the area more dangerous for him and any gang members.

Plummer, seeking sanctuary, rode into the hills. He knew of the fur trading river port of Fort Benton on the headwaters of the Missouri River. It could be a connection back to the states...and possibly home?

FORT BENTON...since 1821

In the Summer of 1859, Captain John La Barge, with a crew of ninety-five men, piloted the *Chippewa*, a 165 foot stern-wheeler from the mouth of the Yellowstone River, up the Mighty Missouri. His destination was 650 miles west to Fort Lewis. It was built in 1821 to accommodate fur traders and traders serving the Indians and later renamed Fort Benton, for Senator Thomas H. Benton, an advocate of expansion to the "Wild West." Captain La Barge ran the *Chippewa* aground on a sandbar only fifteen miles from his destination. Charles P. Chouteau, organizer of the original journey, reported if the river were cleared of obstructions and proper navigation flaws, *"...that the trip from St. Louis to Fort Benton can be easily accomplished within thirty-five days."* On July 2, 1860 the *Chippewa* reached Fort Benton and launched a new river connection to the West! [1]

FORT BENTON...tired Riders

Plummer continued to ride with Charles Reeves and William Ridgley, who had recovered enough to travel. The trio entered Elk City where they separated. Plummer, with Reeves, left Elk City and continued together until they met the Stuart brothers just out of Hell Gate. They spent time at Gold Creek and made friends with the brothers. Between Gold Creek and Fort Benton, Reeves separated from Plummer and rode south to the new gold camp at Bannack on Grasshopper Creek.

On the trail to Fort Benton, Henry Plummer, met with Jack Cleveland, who he knew but did not trust. Plummer was well aware of the history of Cleveland...his real name was John Farnsworth. In July, 1856, he was one of three robbers who broke out of Plummer's jail in Nevada City, California. *(See chapter 2)*. The tension grew with the pairing of two antagonistic individuals, Plummer and Cleveland...they did not trust one-another! [2][3]

Chapter Notes

Note 1. The author's use of "Hanged" vs. "Hung": both forms are used in the context of this story. "Hanged" or "hung," as used in "quotes" of the "Players," has not been changed. In the historical era of the 1860's, there was no declared choice between the two.
Ref: *Random House Webster's Dictionary*, 2nd ed, 1997, pg 590, #4..."To execute by suspending from a gallows, or gibbet." #5..." To suspend by neck until dead."
Ref: *Merriam-Webster Collegiate Dictionary*, 11th ed, 2009, pg 566, "Hanged is most appropriate for official executions, but hung is also used. Eg: ("...gave orders that he should be hung").

Note 2. Jack Cleveland has been noted as "Cunningham" by Edwin Purple in *Perilous Passage* pg 134; and as "John Farnsworth" of Galena, Illinois by Frederick Allen in *A Decent, Orderly Lynching*, pg 73.

Note 3. The first white explorers known to have set foot in Montana were the members of the Lewis and Clark Expedition (1804-06). Fur trappers and traders followed setting up forts to trade with the Indians. The only early trading post to survive as a present-day town was Fort Benton, which was established in 1846 and became an important port on the Missouri River. Roman Catholic Missionaries followed the fur traders and in 1841 established Saint Mary's Mission near present-day Stevensville, believed to be the first permanent settlement in Montana. Trailblazers carved the northern Overland Route to Montana from the east, the Bozeman Trail from the southeast and Mullen Road westward from Fort Benton, the head of Navigation for steamboats on the Missouri.

Gold prospectors flocked in after rich placer deposits were discovered in the 1860's. Montana Territory was established in 1864 with Bannack, on Grasshopper Creek, its first capital and Virginia City, in Alder Gulch, its second. (Ref: Montana, Dorothy M. Johnson, John M. Crowley; *Encyclopedia Britannica*, from Standard Edition, 2003).

Skinner's Saloon, Bannack, Montana

CHAPTER 4
PLUMMER...HOMESICK
Fall, 1862

S.S. EMILIE ARRIVES...with Electa

Fort Benton, was located at the farthest navigable point west on the upper Missouri River. It was built by the government and the Department of Indian Affairs to work with the nearby Indian tribes and upcoming territorial issues and became an important forward base for supplies and passengers into the Northwest Territory. On June 17, 1862, the steamship *Emilie*, a large side-wheeler steered into the riverbank at Fort Benton. It carried supplies and had cabin space for eighty-five first class passengers. On board was a twenty-four year old school teacher from Ohio, James A.Vail. He had been assigned to oversee the government's Indian farm on the Sun River, sixty miles west of Fort Benton. It would be his job to teach and "civilize" the Blackfoot Indians of the area. His wife, Martha Jane, and their two young children Mary and Harvey, accompanied him. Also on board the *Emilie* and entering the wild and wide open Indian country would be young and petite Electa Bryan, James Vail's sister-in-law.

The small, lonely farm was an attempt by the government to educate the large tribe of Blackfoot Indians about crop cultivation and livestock management. To be able to communicate and teach the Indians would also help relieve their war-like attitude.

FRANK THOMPSON...enter a "Bridesmaid"

Also on board was Francis M. Thompson, a well educated banker from the East with his partners in the American Exploring and Mineral Company. Thompson had organized a group of a dozen mining enthusiasts, with plans to seek their fortunes in the new gold fields developing in the Rocky Mountains. News came to Thompson's group about a new gold strike west of Fort Benton. They made preparations to transport their mining supplies and equipment to the area.

The group became friends with the Vail family on the boat trip and joined them in their trip west. They made it to the Sun River where earlier explorers had devised a rope-tow ferry they could use to get their supplies across the river, but the ferry had been damaged and was under water. Together, they repaired and refloated the ferry and successfully transported supplies and equipment across the river. After helping Vails get settled on the government farm at Sun River, Thompson and his mining group headed west to Gold Creek.

Vail and his family were left at the Sun River farm to contend with the hot weather, mosquitoes, rattlesnakes and Indians. The main living quarters for the Vail's, a log cabin, was not well suited for the large family. The Blackfoot Indians were nomadic, a warrior type and looked upon the Vail family and the farm as encroaching. The few rifles and a small cannon on the farm would be of little defense in case of an uprising. With only one Indian helper, and other Indians showing discontent, Vail decided to return to Fort Benton to recruit help.

FORT BENTON...a boat home

Henry Plummer, on the trail to Fort Benton, had plenty of time to ponder leaving the wild, torturous West and to return home to Maine and his family. Could he escape his corrupt past...and not reveal to his family the despicable traits he had learned to use in his life? Could he break away from the saloon devils...the brothels...the killings? Or would they still haunt him? He had a choice, however...he could return to the gold fields. A rich, new gold strike had been found at Bannack on Grasshopper Creek...a long ride south, but a strong temptation!

What might have transpired if Henry Plummer had returned home? He would face a different environment. He would have had a tough time changing his habits...drinking, carousing and abusing women. Gaming tables would also carry a mighty pull on such an avid player as Plummer. The long arm of the law could still reach out for him. His mind, with fears of his past...played Hell with him.

It was early October, 1862, when Plummer and Cleveland arrived at Fort Benton, weary and hungry. They had hoped to find passage down river, but the steamships had already left on their return trip to St. Louis. Indian troubles downstream had the captains of the smaller Mackinaw boats refusing to leave. Any hopes of Plummer heading home and changing his lifestyle were dashed. The passengers disembarking earlier in the summer had left Fort Benton. The fort itself was less than two acres with few buildings and described as nothing more than a livery stable. The trading post of the American Fur Company offered nothing to console the two weary travelers. When James Vail offered them work at the nearby government farm at Sun River they readily accepted. It seemed Plummer would have to spend the winter with Cleveland at Sun River...and do honest work!

Having succeeded in recruiting two willing helpers, Henry Plummer and Jack Cleveland, Vail with his new help hastened back to the farm. He felt more secure with two more helpers, in case of a disturbance from the Indians. Vail showed his new hands a small cabin they would occupy for the winter and put them to work with chores around the farm. The Indian problem diminished.

The western fall was warm, turning the countryside and the river-front trees into a peaceful orange hue. However, the white snow-caps on the western mountains told that winter would soon arrive.

A FIGHT...for love

During their stay at Sun River both Plummer and Cleveland showed an interest in Vail's young sister-in-law, Electa. Cleveland's boisterous attitude against Plummer's more amicable posture gave Plummer a decided upper hand. Electa, frail and demure, was decidedly lonely. With only her sister as companion she was fraught with the desire for friendship. She welcomed Plummer's attention and was overwhelmed by his affection. Whatever Plummer presented, Electa readily accepted... even to his proposal of marriage. Depending on what she could foresee, she felt any life at the Indian farm would be more harsh than a life with Plummer, wherever it might be in this lonely, desolate country.

Plummer envisioned a euphoric future with Electa and could not hesitate putting his plan into motion...a major change! He felt staying the winter at the farm would only delay his future. He told Vail, already with scant rations, it would be an easier winter with two less mouths to feed. He would proceed to Bannack with Cleveland, find provisions and return in the spring for his bride!

The Vails were skeptical, but all they could do was wait. In early November, before snow fall in 1862, Plummer and Cleveland rode off for Bannack, nearly two hundred miles to the south.

LONG RIDE...with questions

It would be a long ride for two men who could not trust each other...especially long, when Plummer had to leave Electa behind. He hoped she would help him void his caustic past. Plummer, not trusting Cleveland, had a major question for him... *"What did you tell her about me!?"* It would probably be the major point of conversation between them as they rode to Bannack. The winter weather started off brisk but mellowed, which made the long ride easier. Crossing the high country in bad weather could prove to be hard on horses, as well as riders.

BANNACK...growing

For several days they followed the Beaverhead River and passed the famous Beaverhead Rock, so named by Sacagawea of the famous Lewis and Clark Expedition of 1805-06. When Plummer and Cleveland finally arrived at Bannack they parted. The antagonistic temperament between them was apparent to the townspeople. Plummer's plan for reform and marriage rested on the silence of Cleveland. In one drunken outburst of Plummer's past history his upcoming wedding would have been destroyed.

Bannack, as well as Yankee Flats, had only a few log cabins and stores along the main street. Grasshopper Creek, originally named Willard's Creek, in honor of Private Alexander Willard, by the Lewis and Clark expedition of 1805, was south of the town running south-east down the gulch. Residents writing home about the town called it "lawless and violent," with plenty of rowdies and sympathizers for both the Union and the South. "Yankee Flats," a sloping hillside meadow south of Grasshopper Creek, housed Unionists including the Fisk Expedition, a wagon train of some 130 weary Minnesotans led overland into the gold country by Army Captain James Liberty Fisk.

On the north side of the creek miners and merchants lived in small log cabins and tents. There were regular evening dances, but the greater part of free time for the miners was spent gambling and drinking, not a good environment for Plummer's plan of reform. Planning for the future, he purchased a plot of ground along the main street for $25 with the hopes of building a cabin suitable for two...him and his bride-to-be.

It was mid-November, 1862, when the Stuart brothers, Granville and James, arrived in Bannack to set up a butcher shop. Plummer had settled himself in preparation of becoming a respectable member of the gold camp society. Plummer had spent time with the Stuart brothers in September at Gold Creek. *(See Chapter one)*. Stuarts had formed a good opinion of Plummer, but were still unaware of his past. As the news of this rich strike spread, Bannack's growth rose. According to notes of Granville Stuart, *"...miners could pan gold out of the sagebrush."* They could pull up sagebrush at the edge of the creek, shake out the roots and find "color" in their pan. [1]

With all the growth in town, the possibility of someone knowing of Plummer's past grew. A saloon keeper in "Yankee Flats" had spent time in San Quentin prison with Plummer...Cyrus Skinner. There were others who knew his history...Bill Bunton, Charley Reeves, Jack Gallagher... all unlucky robbers who had became "pals" and rode with Plummer, but did not care about his sordid past. Yet, others would come as well and Plummer would have more than Jack Cleveland to worry about. He thought about how he would fulfill his hopes of marriage...without his ugly past giving him away. [2]

Some writers and historians questioned his "dream." Was it with Electa, a happenstance meeting, that may interfer with his "original" plan? Some think his original plan was to compose a rogue band of known "ne'er-do-wells" and robbers as his associates...to rob and pillage the wealth of gold from the miners at the newest and richest gold fields of Bannack.

It's doubtful. His love of women, booze and gambling had deteriorated his ability to plan...or to think straight. His unplanned meeting with Cleveland made him recall his lurid past and made him feel like he had to change...to head home?

While at Sun River, luck dealt him a "Queen of Hearts" and changed his hand entirely. He now had to discard the "Joker" he was riding with and find a decent way to support the "Queen." He considered himself the "King," and Bannack would be the next card into holding a "King-high straight."

Chapter Notes

Note 1. Bannack was growing, but not with families. The gold hungry miners did not constitute a "homey" environment for a bride. Henry Plummer was torn between "love" and "riches." It would be a hard choice to make. The long, cold winter would give him time to ponder his future, either with or without ...his prospective bride.

The International Fraternity of the Masonic Lodge of Bannack is shown above. Montana Masonry was born in Bannack. Members of the Historic Lodge, also known as the Montana Vigilantes, helped bring Law and Order to the early Gold Fields of the Territory. The Bannack Masonic Lodge, known as Lodge 3-7-77 held school classes on the first floor of the building and many Vigilante members attended regular meetings on the second floor.

CHAPTER 5
CLEVELAND....DRUNKEN DUEL
PALS shoot up YANKEE FLATS
Winter, 1862-63

DEAD DRUNK...no friends

A local miner, who had converted to ranching, turned up missing while checking on his livestock in Horse Prairie. Soon after, the townspeople noted Jack Cleveland suddenly had plenty of extra gold dust. After the missing rancher's bloody clothes, minus his pouch, were found stuffed in a badger hole along Grasshopper Creek, many in town suspected Cleveland of committing the first killing in Bannack.

On the morning of January 14, 1863, Plummer joined a group of men at the saloon in the Goodrich Hotel. In the group were Harry Phleger, Ivan Moore and Jeff Perkins. They talked or played cards sitting around a warm stove...the weather was cold. The door burst open and Cleveland stumbled in...drunk. He was as usual when drunk...boisterous and swearing. He recognized Perkins and confronted him, *"I've been lookin' for you...You owe me forty dollars!"* Perkins knowing Cleveland's attitude when drunk remained quietly seated and stated the debt had long been paid. Cleveland seemed satisfied...for the moment. After he gazed quizzically around the room, with his hand on his gun, he renewed his angry claim at Perkins. Plummer, in his quiet but demanding voice, told Cleveland, *"...the debt was paid...sit down and be quiet...the matter's finished!"* Red-faced, Cleveland spewed out more threats. Intimidated, Perkins started to leave to get his gun and stop Cleveland's ranting.

Suddenly, Plummer stood up and furiously said to Cleveland, "You son-of-a-bitch...I'm tired of this!" Facing Cleveland, Plummer pulled his pistol, fired one shot into the ceiling to get Cleveland's drunken attention, then fired a second shot into his groin. Cleveland slumped to the floor dumfounded, *"You won't shoot me when I'm down?"* he begged. *"No,"* Plummer answered, *"...Get up!"* As Cleveland struggled to his knees, Plummer put the gun in Cleveland's face and fired... the hot powder seared his face. Plummer quickly shot him again in the chest. Expectedly, it would surely be the deadly shot. Miraculously, writhing on the floor in bloody pain, Jack Cleveland was not yet dead!

The shooting alarmed Edwin Purple, whose shop was just across the street from the Goodrich Hotel. He hurried across the street to the hotel and entered the saloon. Purple saw Cleveland, sprawled on the floor, bleeding and cursing the onlookers, *"Some son-of-a-bitch shoot me!"* He wanted to die...to end the pain!

George Ives and Charlie Reeves hurriedly led Plummer out of the saloon to his cabin. They warned him he could suffer harsh consequences for the shooting...he should seriously think about leaving town.

Harry Phleger, who helped Hank Crawford enforce law and order in the town, summoned Crawford and they carried the wounded Cleveland to Crawford's butcher shop and laid him on the floor. Cleveland, seeking relief from the pain, again pleaded to have someone, *"...shoot me!"*

George Ives returned and entered the shop, looked at Cleveland and said with utter disgust, *"Jack, you'll be in Hell soon! Die like a man... don't make such a damn fuss about it!"* Cleveland gulped and hopelessly mumbled, *"Poor Jack has got no friends. He has got it...I guess he can stand it."* In relief of his pain...he gave up and died. [1]

The shooting brought forth mixed feelings towards Plummer. Some felt, *"He just eliminated a killer,"* and, *"He anticipated Cleveland's intention and fired first."* Others felt differently, *"Cleveland was shot in cold blood!"* and, *"Cruel killing."* ...many others didn't care. No attempt to arrest Plummer was made. Could Plummer now relax... knowing Cleveland would no longer reveal his sordid past ...or had he already talked? Plummer thought it best to take leave of Bannack until the current turmoil quieted.

YANKEE FLATS...shooting

Days after the Cleveland shooting, several angry men raided the Bannock Indian camp south of Yankee Flats. Charles Reeves had recently taken an Indian bride from the Sheepeater tribe of the Bannock Indians, but she ran away from his constant abuse, back to her tribe. When he asked the Tribal Elder for her return...he was denied. Highly irritated over the rebuke, Reeves with friends Charley Moore and William Mitchell, rode by the Indian camp several times, randomly firing shots into the wickiups and teepees. Two Indians, a papoose and a French trader were killed, several others wounded.

The trio beat a retreat to the north, up Rattlesnake Creek, and joined with another rider headed up the gulch...Henry Plummer. However, a posse of four men tracked the band of Indian killers in the snow and soon confronted all of them in a creek-side thicket. Plummer, not the posse's prime interest, did not favor further retreat into the cold, desolate hills. They all surrendered with the stipulation they would be given a trial by jury.

The town wanted a Miner's court or mass jury trial. Earlier threats had been made by Reeves and his cohorts against any juror who would vote to convict them. Nathaniel Langford advised, *"Shall we ignore the agreement made with them by our officers?"* His motion for a trial by jury was soundly voted down. However, after more discussion, it was approved.

A trial was arranged, with a Judge, J.F. Hoyt, and twelve jurors. Langford was chosen as one of the jurors. Hank Crawford was appointed sheriff, giving him authority he had lacked before, and two lawyers agreed to act as counsel. Crawford, a relentless, law-abiding townsman and shopkeeper, who although not elected or designated as sheriff, had tried to keep some semblance of law, as yet unwritten in Bannack. The court, held in a large log building, was attended by a large crowd of armed and angry townspeople.[2]

Plummer, being tried for killing Cleveland, testified that Cleveland, also known as Farnsworth, had a grudge against him dating back to his duty as Sheriff in California. The jury was satisfied...and Plummer was quickly exonerated of shooting Cleveland.

The case against Reeves and partners in the Indian shooting at Yankee Flats was taken more seriously. The residents feared the Indians after being attacked would gather and seek bloody revenge upon the town.

Mitchell was acquitted of any killing...he could show he had not fired his gun during the shooting. For taking part in the melee, however, he was banished from the gulch. The acting counsel for Moore and Reeves argued an instance in California in 1862, in which Snake and Bannock Indians rallied and killed friends and relatives of the defendants...he hoped it would provoke leniency for his clients. Townspeople thought Moore and Reeves should hang! Fierce intimidation by friends of the prisoners took its toll. They shouted, brandished knives and pointed guns at both the Judge and jury. The jury vote was close, eleven to one... not guilty. Langford cast the only vote for hanging. With further urging and fierce deliberation by Langford, the jury reconsidered...guilty! Their just and only penalty...banishment!

Moore and Reeves were taken north to Deer Lodge and told to exit the area in the spring, when weather permitted crossing the snow-capped Rocky Mountains and not to come back. If they were found within six-hundred miles of Bannack they were to be hanged! Later, Mitchell returned to Bannack, sick, bedraggled and hungry. Mitchell was allowed to stay, but nobody seemed to care. The townsmen then revoked the banishment against Moore and Reeves. They came back to Bannack, bitter and resentful...with revenge on their minds!

41

YOU ARE GUILTY...and you are dead

There were two cases of reckless and wanton killings...with five people dead and no one essentially punished. It was felt by many townspeople of Bannack a grave injustice had taken place...especially among those townsmen with greater societal bonding, such as churchgoers and members of the Masonic Lodge.

In his book *Vigilante Days and Ways*, N.P. Langford bitterly wrote about the incident, *"Thus, the first scene in the drama, which had been ushered in by such a bloody prologue,* (the shooting) *terminated in the broadest farce* (the trial)." Plummer and his gang decreed death...to all who had participated in the trial!

Langford continued, *"...within five months after the trial, not more than seven of the twenty-seven men who participated in it as judge, prosecutor, sheriff, witnesses, and jurors, were left alive in the territory. Eight or nine are known to have been killed by some of the band, and others fled to avoid a like fate."* Threats of revenge by gang members took a dreaded toll on those who sought justice in the area.[3]

A MASONIC FUNERAL...begin an ending

In the spring of 1863, a respected citizen of Bannack, William H. Bell, died of Mountain Fever. It was the first natural death in the Bannack gold field. Before his death he requested, as a Mason, that he be buried with full Masonic ceremonies.

All local members of the order were requested to meet at C. J. Miller's cabin on Yankee Flats for the ceremonies that evening. The huge number of area members that responded surprised both Miller and Langford. They had to move the meeting to larger quarters and it was past midnight before proper forms of recognition were completed. After the meeting, because of the large turnout, it was, *"...virtually understood that early application should be made for authority to open a lodge. In the meantime, we agreed to hold frequent meetings."*

William Bell was buried the next day. Nathaniel Langford conducted funeral ceremonies with a large congregation of members assembled, plus a group of curious onlookers. *"Among this number might be seen many whose daily lives were filled with deeds of violence and crime who perhaps at the moment might be meditating murder and robbery... all armed with revolvers and bowie-knives...."* Langford further wrote, *"They learned from what they saw, that here was an association, bound together by bonds of brotherly love, that would stand by and protect all its members in the hour of danger."*

It was only the beginning of the end! The Henry Plummer gang, who forced a purge of violence upon the citizenry of Bannack, would feel the crushing brunt of this "association!" *"...the ruffians who had marked them (Masons) for ultimate destruction felt that a new, formidable adversary had thrown it-self across their bloody pathway."*

The burial of their member was finished, and the members went home, but their work had just begun. *"...the Masons met often for counsel. Among them there was no lack of confidence, and very soon they began to consider measures necessary for their protection."*

Their meetings became more frequent and more noticed by those who would soon feel the brunt of their force. To allay the curiosity of their adversaries, *"...They were quietly told that the Masons met to prepare for organizing a lodge. This threw them off their guard, and they continued their lawless course."* With the news that a lodge was in the making, *"Plummer expressed publicly a strong desire to become a Mason...He succeeded in convincing some members of the order..."* he was not a murderous character, and that previous killings were actuated by reason of self-defense. However, he still could not convince any member of the Masons to recommend him for membership!

Langford also wrote, *"It is a remarkable fact that the roughs were restrained, by their fear of the Masonic fraternity, from attacking its individual members. Of the one hundred and two persons murdered by Henry Plummer's gang, not one was a Mason."* It is further noted by Langford, *"...that every Mason in these trying hours adhered steadfastly to his principles."* He continued, *"...not one of all that band of desperadoes who expiated a life of crime upon the scaffold, had ever crossed the threshold of a lodge room. The irregularities of their lives, their love of crime, and their recklessness of law, originated in the evil associations and corrupt influences of a society over which neither Masonry nor Religion had ever exercised the least control. The retribution which finally overtook them had its origin in principles traceable to that stalwart morality which is the offspring of Masonic and Religious institutions."* [4]

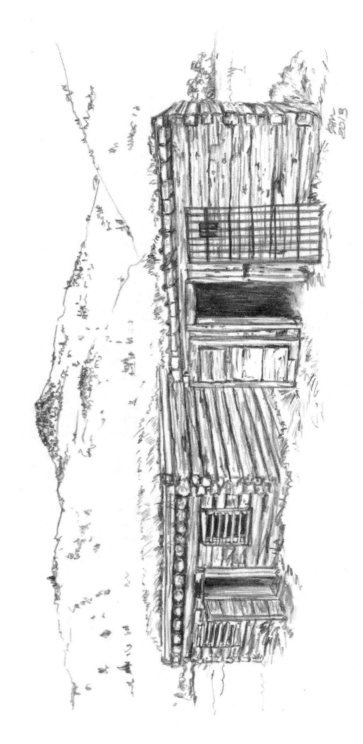

Bannack Jail
Bannack, Montana

CHAPTER 6
PLUMMER prods SHERIFF CRAWFORD
Late Winter, 1863

KILLER...not true

There had been no evidence of illegal activities attributed to Plummer in Bannack, other than his association with the "rough" crowd. The previous shooting on Yankee Flats depicted a known and willing connection with derelicts. Many of these shady individuals acknowledged they knew Plummer in California or Idaho, but said nothing of his past, other than his being fast and deadly with a pistol. He had killed five men up to this point, but all were reported as "self-defense," and questionable! Plummer stated, *"I confess that the bad associations which I formed in California and Nevada have adhered to me ever since. I was forced in sheer self-defense on different occasions, to kill five men there...and of course was undeservedly denounced as a desperado and murderer. This is not true...."*

Plummer eliminated the boisterous voice of Cleveland, declaring innocence of any crime. He was free to walk the streets of town without doubt or worry...except for one man...Sheriff Crawford. Could Cleveland have said anything to Crawford on his deathbed? Paranoia held Plummer's mind and haunted him! He decided he must kill Crawford before bringing his "bride-to-be" back to Bannack! She must not learn of his lurid past from anyone but him...if at all.

PRODDING...all staged

Meeting Crawford on the street, Plummer continually prodded him about what Cleveland may have said to him. Crawford denied Cleveland had told him anything. Plummer would not believe him and did not relax. He knew Crawford was lying and would have to lure him into an altercation where shooting him would be justified.

In a staged scenario Plummer's stooge tried to pick a fight with Crawford in a saloon, but not with guns...with fists! Crawford unbuckled his gun belt, set it aside and slapped the man hard in the face. Stunned, the man drew a hidden gun from his coat. Crawford, not a coward, grabbed the man's throat and pulled the gun from his grip. Plummer lunged into the fracas and snatched the gun from Crawford. However, before Plummer could do anything Harry Phleger stepped in, with guns drawn and leveled at Plummer...and stopped the fight. Later the barkeeper admitted he knew Plummer had deliberately staged the ruckus.

Henry Phleger, long time friend of Hank Crawford, maintained a defensive air about Plummer. A freighter, Phleger, had several teamsters working for him. He told them, *"If Plummer, or any of his associates comes for me, and I make the first shot and you fail to make the second...I will shoot you!....Just remember that!"* [1]

Later, meeting Crawford in a saloon, Plummer called him a coward, swore at him and dared him to fight. He pushed Crawford into the street where he dared Crawford to pull his gun. Crawford calmly said he had no cause...he never had cause to pull his gun on any man. Plummer was furious, *"Pull it!"* he demanded. *"No man can say I never gave you a chance."* Plummer could hardly hold back...the time had come, *"Pull it and cock it and I won't go for mine until you say 'fire.'"* Crawford knew how little chance Plummer would give him...the slightest movement toward his gun belt would mean death. He looked directly at Plummer and slowly shook his head in stubborn denial. *"You're a damn coward!"* Plummer cursed, frustrated in an attempt to get Crawford to fight. *"Fight... like a man now, or by God, I'll shoot you down like a dog! I'll give you two hours and then I'll kill you on sight!"* Plummer, a gambler, had lost the cool edge of his temper!

To show Plummer he was the braver of the two, Crawford slowly put his hand on Plummer's shoulder and said quietly, *"If that's your game, Plummer, the quicker you play it, the worse for you."* He looked into Plummer's dark snake-like eyes and said, *"I'll give you a fair target."* He turned, with his back to Plummer and calmly walked away. Plummer, stunned, watched Crawford leave... he knew he had lost to a better man. With his pride buckled, Plummer had a major reason to kill Hank Crawford.

PLUMMER'S RAGE.....clouds his mind

Again, only hours later, Plummer met Crawford in Peabody's saloon. Plummer had several of his armed men with him. Phleger offered to buy everyone a drink, but was refused. One gang member faced Crawford and called him a coward, that he was afraid to fight Plummer. Plummer stepped between them and handed his man a revolver. The crowd backed away afraid of being hit in a shooting.

Crawford turned to Phleger, *"Harry, I suppose these men have come to kill me. You are my only friend, and I'll make you a present of my six-shooter. I suppose I've got to die."* Plummer lunged forward in an attempt to snatch the gun from Phleger, but was pushed back. Phleger pulled a second pistol from his belt and ready to fire, he said to Crawford, *"Come on, Hank, let's get out of this."* And once again Harry

Phleger held Plummer and his cohorts at bay while he and Crawford backed out into the street. When they reached his cabin, Crawford broke down. Facing Plummer was getting to be too much...but he knew it was not yet finished.

Plummer concocted another scenario. To have cause for killing Crawford, Plummer spread rumors that Crawford told everyone he had been sleeping with Catherine, a drunken Indian mistress. In the eyes of the townsfolk, Plummer's "lie" should surely create enough cause for him to kill Crawford...and not be charged.

Two days after the incident in Peabody's saloon, Plummer looking for Crawford, accidently met Harry Phleger and challenged him to a shootout in the street. Phleger replied sedately, *"No thank you, Plummer, I'm not looking around for anyone to shoot this morning..."*

Meanwhile Crawford, with a loaded pistol, was determined to put an end to his torment. He searched for Plummer...with the dire purpose of killing him. Plummer, however, sent a message to Crawford that said they should drop all hostilities and just meet as strangers, without anger...a staged ploy by Plummer to kill Crawford.

"Tell Plummer," Crawford warily said, *"That trick is too shallow. I know him...one of us must die or leave the camp!"* [2]

Plummer waits to ambush Hank Crawford.

CRAWFORD...bad shot

Soon after, it was learned by friends of Crawford, Plummer had planned to shoot him in the doorway of his butcher shop. On the morning of March 6, 1863, Plummer stood outside Crawford's shop, with a double-barreled shotgun. He leaned on a wagon sitting in the street and waited for Crawford. For a good steady shot, he braced himself on the wagon wheel, but Crawford was not in his shop.

Prior to Plummer's arrival, Crawford had been invited to have coffee in Jim Harby's restaurant across the road from the parked wagon. While he drank his coffee, Crawford was told by Frank Ray, *"Plummer is on the prowl,"* and gave him Buz Caven's double barreled rifle. *"Use it!"*

Crawford took the rifle and left by the back door of the restaurant. He slowly walked up the side of the cabin toward the street. He saw Plummer leaning on the wagon with his back to him. Crawford rested the rifle on a protruding log on the front of the restaurant, steadied himself, took aim and fired at the unsuspecting Plummer!

The rifle ball hit Plummer just above the elbow of the right arm, traveled down the forearm tearing up muscle, bone and tissue. Stunned, Plummer regained his footing, turned around and saw Crawford. He stood erect and shouted, *"Fire away, you cowardly...!"* Crawford hurriedly fired a second shot, but missed! Plummer in agony walked away, holding onto his shotgun. In that distinct moment, as he faced eminent death, Plummer's mettle gained him undue admiration.

Crawford, shaken by the shooting, entered Edwin Purple's store just down the street. Pale, he said he, *"...was not used to the rifle!"* and questioned how he, *"...had shot so wild."* Bill Goodrich, in Purple's store, tried to convince Crawford to, *"Load up and go out and finish the job!"* Purple advised Crawford to get over his excitement before he attempted another shot. He said, *"...he could not have hit the side of a house, forty paces off!"* Crawford took Purple's advice and hid from Plummer and his cohorts for several days, knowing he faced imminent death.

Tended by several of his close friends at his cabin, Plummer was enraged at being ambushed by Crawford. Unaware how badly the shot had damaged his arm, his anger must have acted as a pain-killer. Thinking only of revenge, and not the pain, Plummer sent word to Crawford to meet him in fifteen days to fight, *"...with Bowie knives...or pistols...as you choose!"*

DOCTOR!...don't lose your head

Dr. Jerome Glick, a noted surgeon with plenty of practice on gunshot wounds, attended to Plummer's wounds and advised amputation of the arm. Plummer staunchly refused, with support from friends, who threatened, *"...fix him or die...!"* Plummer could not afford losing another hand, his left one already disabled earlier in life. Suddenly "Old" Tex and Bill Hunter burst in with a shotgun pointed at the Doctor. Hunter said, *"I just thought that I'd tell you...if Plummer dies from the operation...I'm going to shoot the top of your head off!"* Dr. Glick proceeded with due caution...and a "forced" dedication to his patient. Plummer's arm continued to swell and he began the onset of fever.

Doctor Glick, worried his patient had little chance of recovery, prepared for the worse. He ordered a horse ready and waiting at the stable for his escape if Plummer did not pull through the surgery. He slept with his boots and spurs on. However, a favorable change came about and Plummer...and the Doctor... pulled through. Crawford's bullet caused considerable damage to Plummer's right arm, ending lodged in his wrist, which disabled the use of his shooting arm and hand.

Fearing for his life against Plummer and his roughs, Henry "Hank" Crawford decided the odds against him were too great and hurriedly left Bannack. He rode to Fort Benton where he boarded a Mackinaw boat and returned to his home in Wisconsin. He eventually married an old sweetheart. He never returned to Bannack, but later moved to Virginia City with his wife and raised two children. [3]

DOCTOR'S ORDERS...keep quiet

It was not an uncommon task for Dr. Glick to repair gunshot wounds on Plummer's associates. On an earlier occasion Plummer asked the doctor to accompany him to a hideout where they met several men with blackened or masked faces. He was asked to attend to the wounded leg of Billy Terwiliger. The doctor recognized several of the men. On their return ride, after the wound had been repaired, Plummer suddenly whirled in front of the Doctor with his gun in his face and said, *"Now you know all. These are my men. I'm their chief. If you breathe a word of what you've seen, I'll murder you!"* [4]

Chapter Notes

Note 1. The formation of the "association" (Masonic Lodge) would prove to be a major
note in the Vigilante History of Montana and Henry Plummer. Much of that history
has been held only in the annals of secrecy of the Masonic Lodge. Only recently has
any declaration been made of those historical facts ever reaching the public. However,
the Masonic membership of the era (1860's) would prove to be a major player in the
formation of Montana's history.

CHAPTER 7
PART ONE
MARRIAGE & MURDER
ELECTA MYSTERY
Late Spring, Summer, 1863

ELECTION...a need for Lawmen

At a meeting with townspeople, Walter Dance as President of the Bannack Mining District, gained agreement from the people that an election should be held for a team to enforce some form of law for the growing town. This election would be Bannack's first step to form order in the community. There were no guidelines for such an election, no control of who would be eligible to vote, or proper recording of the outcome. There was a lack of "legality" to any formal elections in this portion of the newly formed Idaho Territory. (Which contained present day Montana). It still lacked a Chief Justice, as well as an established system for law and order.

At an earlier election, in May, 1856, Plummer had faced a similar situation for the position of Marshall of Nevada City, California. He would again face the public voters for a job in law enforcement in Bannack...but he now had the experience he lacked before!

On May 24, 1863, Henry Plummer was chosen over his opponent, by a paper thin majority, not unlike the earlier California election. The movement toward formation of a citizenry with controls of legality and order, were slow and tedious...not to mention...possibly corrupt! "Swarms of outsiders" flowed into Bannack from surrounding areas and nearby mining camps to cast a vote. Suspicions rose later that many of those "unfamiliar" faces were friends of Henry Plummer and they had voted more than once.

After being elected, Plummer approached Nathanial Langford and asked for a fair chance to do the job, *"I will show you that I can be a good man among men. This is a new life before me."* Langford was not thoroughly convinced.

A SHERIFF...turned Lover

With a badly damaged gun-hand, Plummer was handicapped in his capacity as sheriff and the ability to wield power over his men...his cohorts in business. Before Plummer left to attend his wedding in Sun

River he appointed Jack Gallagher, Ned Ray and Buck Stinson to act as deputies in Bannack, with D.H. Dillingham as chief deputy. None were experienced in law enforcement and all lacked a good knowledge of order..."Who's boss?"

Plummer as the new Sheriff, with his recent declaration to Langford, should be showing greater responsibility to the townspeople, but who does he saddle up with?...a pair of prison escapees, Cyrus Skinner and Charles Ridgley, plus a new man in town...Edward Richardson. Richardson, however, had been involved in a couple of shootings and was wanted for murder in Carson City.

Plummer's mining claims were doing well, he had a respected position in the town and he was about to be married to a respectable girl...but, he continued to associate with thieves and killers?

ALDER GULCH...good "color"

As Plummer prepared to leave Bannack to marry Electa Bryan in Sun River, a bedraggled miner, William Fairweather, came to town to buy mining supplies. Half the town of Bannack followed him back to the newest gold strike in the Territory at Alder Gulch, 70 miles away on the "Stinking Water" (Ruby) River.

Six prospectors, including William Fairweather and John Edgar, struck gold at Alder Gulch on May 26, 1863. They went to Bannack for needed supplies after they staked twelve claims for what would prove to be the richest gold strike the country has ever known. Fairweather and Edgar left Bannack on June 2, followed by a large hoard of hungry gold miners. The exodus from Bannack to the new gold strike greatly shrank the population and hurt business.

MARRIAGE...maybe

Meanwhile Frank Thompson, after spending the winter in San Francisco, returned to Vail's Indian Farm at Sun River, west of Fort Benton. Thompson expected a confirmation letter from his brother in St. Louis telling him his supplies of mining equipment had been shipped and when he could expect them. He had hoped they would be on the steamship *Shreveport*, coming up the Missouri River to Fort Benton.

The Vail's were glad to see Thompson, but they had a problem...they were distraught over Electa's upcoming marriage to Henry Plummer. They hoped Thompson would be able to convince her to reconsider. Thompson, aware Plummer had killed Cleveland in Bannack, urged Electa to return home for a while, but did not tell her of Plummer's killing. He had hoped a decided change in Plummer's lifestyle would take place and they could reunite in the fall.

After days of resisting, Electa relented to Thompson's advice and packed her bags for the journey home. Electa planned to board the steamship due to dock soon.

The *S.S. Shreveport* had left St. Louis on April 19, hopefully carrying Vail's family Pastor, who had originally recruited James Vail to manage the Indian farm and was to perform the wedding at Sun River. It was expected he would be aboard the next steamship.

On June 2, 1863, Plummer arrived at the farm at Sun River for the wedding. Frank Thompson had never met Henry Plummer. He later wrote, *"When I saw him I could but wonder if this could be the young desperado whom people so much feared,"* and who *"...seemed devoted to Miss Bryan."*

Electa Bryan, upon Plummer's arrival, changed her mind about leaving and renewed her desire for nuptials. Even Thompson was enamored by Plummer's suave demeanor. The Vails abandoned their objection to the marriage, but requested the couple wait for the arrival of their Pastor from Iowa. The *S.S. Shreveport* had been scheduled to dock at Fort Benton shortly, but due to the drought, the river had low water and the ship ran aground two-hundred miles down-river at Cow Island. It had unloaded the passengers and all freight onto the river bank. The relief of the extra weight made the steamship more buoyant and navigable in the low river and it returned to St. Louis. Passengers were highly disturbed at the ship's Captain, having been disembarked short of their destination and having to travel, as they could, overland into Fort Benton.

After two weeks at Sun River, waiting for Vail's family Pastor to arrive, Plummer grew restless and insisted the wedding ceremony should proceed. James Vail knew of the ship's problem and realized their Pastor would not arrive. He requested services of a cleric, Father Joseph Minatre, from nearby Saint Peter's Jesuit Mission and on June 20, 1863, Electa Bryan and Henry Plummer were married.

Young Joseph Swift who had worked on the ranch served as best man for Plummer. Frank Thompson filled in as "bridesmaid" in place of Martha Jane Vail, who chose not to participate ... she fervently disliked Plummer. After the wedding they enjoyed a meal of Buffalo hump and cornbread. The newlyweds used the farm "ambulance," a four horse wagon with cover, for their honeymoon ride to married life in Bannack. [1]

MYSTERY...lonely?...why?

Being in unfamiliar country, on a desolate Government ranch, Electa felt desperately lonely. She felt being married to Henry Plummer would be a gratifying and fruitful change in her otherwise demeaning, unromantic life. She hoped that Plummer, a handsome gentleman, would be her springboard to a happy married life. She hoped he would become closer and appreciate her more.

After a short time at her new home in Bannack, she found her new husband had greater interests...Gold...and Power! He had a personal ego Electa did not notice in Sun River...his need to *"control."* Electa, being well-raised, a "Prim and Prissy" woman, found her husband delving into activities she did not expect to be a part of her married life.

Electa had been enamored by this handsome cowboy, with whom she expected to ride off into a happy married life. She had no real concept of the rugged country in the west, the lure of gold, the killings and the Hurdy-Gurdy houses! She found she was being left alone too much, while her husband tended to his interests "away from home!" She was stuck! He became a burr in her hopes...instead of being a faithful partner!

Electa's life, although demeaning at her home in Iowa, became more frustrating than she had hoped to face in Bannack...with Henry Plummer. She had been disappointed twice before in her struggle for a new life and love...*she gave up!*

On September 2, 1863, less than three months after her wedding in Sun River, Electa decided to leave Bannack...and Henry Plummer! Her distraught husband rode on horseback alongside the coach. It was a shock to her sister's family. Questions arose in the community why she wanted to leave, but no one could give any answers. On September 6, during their trip south, Electa with Henry Plummer riding horseback, met and talked to a large group on the eastern bank of the Snake River. The wagon train, headed in the opposite direction...north to Bannack, carried Sidney Edgerton, Wilbur Sanders and their families. They were originally headed to Lewiston, the newly named Capitol of the new Idaho Territory, but due to colder weather and oncoming winter, decided to go to the closest town, Bannack. [2]

SOLUTION?...who knows

Why did Electa decide to pack up and leave her husband? She had been enamored with Plummer. What made her change her mind in such a short time?...a great mystery enters into the Plummer marriage.

Electa told her friend, Frank Thompson, she was *"lonely!"* Plummer was away for long periods, but friendly neighbors were decent and nearby. Also, her sister and family, had recently moved to Bannack from Sun River.

Frank Thompson, someone who understood Electa's problems, would provide a possible answer. He realized she lived in a desolate country, without family, and not enough time with her new husband. Plummer, always busy with his other problems, left her alone. With a husband, as Sheriff, most neighbors were hesitant to provide close, friendly company.

Was she pregnant...and wanted better care than the country doctor who fixed Plummer's arm? There was no record of a child...or a miscarriage. Had she found out about her husband's lurid past...his killings? Would Plummer be willing to follow her home and start a new life in Iowa?

Frank Thompson offered an answer to Electa's problem of loneliness. He wrote later, *"Mrs. Plummer told me that Mr. Plummer was away from home so much attending to his duties as sheriff, that she, with his consent, had concluded to go to her home in Iowa, and he was to meet her there in the Fall."*

Frank Thompson lived with the Vail Family in Bannack. Joseph Swift, Electa and Henry Plummer lived nearby and also boarded at Vail's cabin. Thompson had suspicions of Plummer's activities, but the two were friendly. Electa trusted and confided in Thompson about her feelings towards Plummer.

GOVERNMENT FARM...a failure

Thompson spent time helping Vails on the farm at Sun River, while waiting for everyone to arrive for the wedding. For Swift's winter's work at the farm, James Vail paid him with six oxen. Thompson and Swift decided to work as partners and prepared to start for Bannack.

The Vails had not received money to keep the farm in operation...the cows had gone dry, supplies of sugar and flour ran out...and the drought devastated all of the planted crops. Vail and his wife thought it a good idea to abandon the farm and follow Thompson and Swift to Bannack where they could reunite with Electa and start over.

Upon arriving at Deer Lodge, Thompson finally received the long awaited notice from his brother in St. Louis, confirming six tons of supplies were on the Steamship *Shreveport*. Swift sold his oxen at Johnny Grant's ranch and together they continued to Bannack to find a store to sell their load of supplies...which were left on the banks of the great Missouri River at Cow Island.

Because of the new gold strike at Alder Gulch, the area became overrun with gold hungry prospectors...which brought more robberies, more holdups and shootings. Thompson called the area, *"...a reign of terror!"*

Later that summer in September, Thompson met newcomers to Bannack. Thompson had found a suitable location in Bannack and set up a shop to sell the supplies. A wagon train, diverted by the oncoming cold weather, carried the appointed Chief Justice for the new Idaho Territory, Sidney Edgerton. With him came his nephew, a young lawyer from Ohio, Wilbur Fisk Sanders, and their families. While looking for someplace to stay, they met Thompson, talked about their arduous trip and they became good friends. [3]

PART TWO
DILLINGHAM MURDER
Late Spring, Summer, 1863

DILLINGHAM...appointment recalled

While the new Sheriff Plummer was away from Bannack for his marriage in Sun River, he assigned four men to act as deputies. Three of them, Stinson, Ray and Gallagher, were loyalists to Plummer. But Chief Deputy, D. H. Dillingham, tended to business as the public thought a lawman should, not necessarily as Sheriff Plummer had planned. The newly appointed Chief Deputy had suspicions of Buck Stinson, another appointed deputy. Stinson had traveled a great deal with Hayes Lyons between Bannack and the new strike at Alder Gulch. Dillingham confided to a friend earlier, *"...I have overheard them, talking over their plans, and I am going after them."* If he had reported this to Plummer, it would mean a sudden "termination" of his job.

A friend of Dillingham, "Wash" Stapleton, had planned a trip to Alder Gulch. Dillingham warned him about the chance of robbery and the reckless acts of Stinson. His warning to Stapleton, unknowingly, traveled back to Stinson.

Stapleton decided to make the trip anyway, but was stopped along the way by Lyons. When asked if he had been warned that someone intended to rob him, Stapleton denied any such knowledge. He was allowed to continue unharmed.

Knowing about the warning, Lyons and Stinson made immediate plans for the assassination of the informer, Dillingham, in Virginia City.

THREE SHOOTERS...one victim

Shortly after the marriage in Fort Benton, on the morning of Monday, June 29, 1863, Dr. William L. Steele, President of the new mining district of Alder Gulch, held hearings on several disputed mining claims in a makeshift building along the creek side in Alder Gulch. Charley Forbes, acted as recorder for the hearings. He was young, intelligent and clean-cut, but no one knew his background.

Stinson and Lyons burst into the wickiup, interrupted the session, and briskly said Dillingham had just rode into town. Forbes jumped up and left with the two men. Shortly after, Forbes, Stinson and Lyons, confronted Dillingham, called him a liar and traitor to Plummer and boldly shot him in the leg, then in the chest, killing him. The shooting brought a crowd, including Dr. Steele, who told Deputy Jack Gallagher to arrest all three and confiscate their weapons. The crowd insisted on an immediate trial. A wagon was pulled up to act as an outdoor courtroom.

Dr. Steele asked two onlookers from the crowd to act with him as Judges. Several witnesses told they heard Forbes call out, *"Don't shoot, Don't shoot!"* The confused witnesses claimed Forbes shot Dillingham, while others said he did not. Deputy Gallagher, who had conveniently collected all the guns, discreetly reloaded Forbes pistol, then openly examined the guns before the crowd and said Forbes' pistol had not been fired.

YOUNG FORBES...not so clean cut

The selected Judges then decided a trial for the three shooters should be held before the enraged crowd. Henry Percival Adams (H.P.A.) Smith, an oratorical genius when not drunk, acted as Counsel for Forbes. At noon the next day, Stinson and Lyons were both declared guilty by the "court." The crowd favored the clean-cut, straight-forward Forbes and acquitted him. The crowd loudly called that Stinson and Lyons be immediately hung! A makeshift gallows was erected and two graves were dug. However, had they known the history of "Young Charley Forbes," the trial may have taken a different turn and one more grave, for Forbes, would have been dug!

Charley Forbes, an alias, was really Ed Richardson, from Grass Valley, California. It was thought his father had been a respected Judge in Northern California. However, he had been jailed as a teenager and served time in San Quentin prison.

Forbes (Richardson) had also been arrested and jailed over a fatal shooting in Carson City, but soon escaped. Richardson had fled to Bannack where he shot and killed a man in a bar fight. Although drinking and crime plagued him, it was not known if Counsel Smith even knew of his criminal history...or cared!

A wagon carried stone-faced Buck Stinson with Hayes Lyons, who constantly sobbed for mercy, towards the newly constructed gallows. The sheriff of Alder Gulch questioned the crowds' determination about hanging Stinson and Lyons, especially when their partner Forbes had been cleared of any crime. He called for the crowd to vote again. The voice vote again was unsure...with still no firm resolution...until Deputy Jack Gallagher stepped forward, waved his pistol in the air and shouted, *"Let them go! They're cleared!"* Amid the confused crowd, Lyons and Stinson cast the final vote...they spotted a nearby Indian pony, seized it and riding double, galloped out of town. Some say they even had the audacity to stop and urinate in the newly dug graves meant for their burial! No one pursued them. One of the guards looked at the newly constructed and unused gallows and stated, *"There stands a monument of disappointed justice."* [4]

Years later, Dr. William L. Steele reflected it had been Forbes who shot Dillingham with cold calculation, crying, *"Don't Shoot!"* Gallagher unnoticed during the crowd's distraction, had reloaded Forbes pistol. However, Gallagher later disclosed that the pistol he reloaded belonged to Stinson, not Forbes! Forbes was acquitted. Later while in jail with Stinson, Lyons declared he had been the shooter of Dillingham.

Shortly after the trial Charley Forbes slipped off into the oblivion of the west, unless...as some believed...he beat a trail back to Bannack and resumed his true identity of Edward Richardson. Forbes was not on the Vigilante hanging list, and neither was Richardson.

After the Dillingham shooting, Nathanial P. Langford wrote Charley Forbes had, *"...fallen victim to the vengeance of his comrades for... securing for himself a separate trial."* Langford's belief was based on Plummer's earlier declaration that Richardson (Forbes), *"... in a quarrel with Moore at the Big Hole River, Forbes was killed."* Confirmation of his shooting came later from friends of the killer... *"Moore,"* who also burned both his victim's body and that of his horse... to ashes! [5]

Deputy D.H. Dillingham had enforced the law as he felt it should be, but not as proposed by Plummer. His appointment was "recalled," as Plummer had most likely ordered. Plummer could care less Dillingham had not carried out his devious orders. His body was one of the first to be buried in Virginia City's Cemetery Hill.

Thus, townspeople witnessed another open shooting, with the killers brazenly riding off to freedom. They felt justice had not been ardently served...citizens' desires grew for something other than Plummer's form of "law and order."

TRIVIA NOTES....on respect

Langford and Judge Dance were walking together one day earlier when they saw Plummer approaching them. Judge Dance instinctively pulled out his Bowie knife and started whittling on a piece of wood. Plummer stopped and asked, *"Judge, why do you always begin to whittle when you meet me?"* The Judge answered with stern indignation in his voice, *"Because, sir, I never intend that you shall get the advantage of me. You know my opinion of you and your friends. I will not be shot down like a dog by any of you, if I can help it."* A prominent voice regarding the Bannack Sheriff is loud and clear! [6]

Chapter Notes

Note 1. The local Indians, Shoshone, called the water in the Ruby River, Pasamari, which means "stinking water." It is believed there were sulphur deposits nearby which entered the river.

Note 2. Years later, Electa rejoined the Vails in Vermillion, Dakota Territory, where she became a teacher. In January of 1874, she married and gave birth to two sons. (There is an unconfirmed report a third child died at birth.) She died in 1912, and was buried in Wakonda, South Dakota. From those who knew her, she spoke very little publicly about her short marriage

Note 3. Following the shooting of Dillingham, Deputy Gallagher quietly reloaded Forbes' pistol, because he was sure Forbes was the shooter. Later the Judge claimed it was Stinson as the shooter. And later yet, when Lyons was in jail, he confessed to the shooting! It is hard to determine...Who was it?

Note 4. Father Peter John De Smet, a Belgian born Priest, in his travels through the Northwest Territories had many times passed through Saint Peter's Mission, in his efforts to help Indian tribes, especially the Sioux, and to establish a permanent Mission in the Northwest. In June of 1862, the steamship, *Spread Eagle* had docked at Fort Benton and Father De Smet enjoyably delivered to Saint Peter's Mission a desperately needed boatload of supplies; food for nearly a year, tools, picks and shovels, several plows, an ambulance, bedding, clothes, etc. Most of all, the Jesuits at Saint Peter's appreciated and welcomed the gift of cloth underwear...to replace the chafing buckskin they were forced to wear when their traditional black gowns became too worn and tattered.

"Coming down a steep pitch, one of the wheels on Mr Chipman's wagon...broke a number of spokes, and we are obliged to stop." (Page 63)

CHAPTER 8
COLONEL SANDERS reaches BANNACK
Summer, 1863

LEWIS and CLARK...A look into the past

Early in the start of the 19th Century, Congress assigned the exploration of the vast land of the Louisiana Purchase to Captains Meriwether Lewis and William Clark. They had hoped to find a trade route across this northwest country to encourage business from the Asian markets. Lewis and Clark started from St. Louis and traveled by boat, horseback and by foot across this multi-terrained country to the west coast of Oregon and back. Their arduous trip started in the Spring of 1804, and carried them to the Pacific Coast until their return in the Fall of 1806. They were not searching for gold, silver or copper...they were just "looking." They recorded what they saw into the annals of American history.

In the next 55 years this expansive Northwest Territory grew and became populated. In 1862, the once vast Washington Territory was to be split once more by Congress to form a new Territory, which would contain present day Idaho, Montana and Wyoming and was called *Idaho Territory*. Inhabitants came from the gold fields of California and surrounding areas looking to strike it rich in the new gold camps. Small camps grew up around the new strikes...they lived as long as the "color" flowed....then they died.

JOB OPENING....in the Wild West

Earlier, in July of 1862, a new gold camp sprouted from one of the richest finds in the country. John White and his companions from Colorado found a rich placer strike on Grasshopper Creek...and Bannack was born! The gold from the *"Grasshopper diggin's"* was rated as being 99 to 99.5% pure. Most strikes were only 95% pure.

By early 1863, the horse trails of the small town of Bannack became platted streets with tents and wickiups, log cabins, shops and churches and a population close to 1,000 restless miners. [1]

President Lincoln, in early 1863, appointed Sidney Edgerton as the Chief Justice of the new Idaho Territory. Edgerton's purpose would be to prepare a system of Justice for the growing area with laws and enforcement.

Edgerton, elected to Congress in 1858 from Ohio, was a well known attorney, a self made man, who attended Cincinnati Law School. He opposed slavery and ardently supported the idea of a transcontinental railway. He accepted the Presidential appointment and promptly prepared to leave for the wilderness of the new Territory. Edgerton's party included his nephew, a young attorney, Wilbur Fisk Sanders.

SANDERS...to play a role in history

Wilbur Sanders showed numerous abilities and an always alert, quizzical mind that sought answers. In his youth he worked in the fields on his father's farm as well as neighboring farms. His earnings, from neighbors, were kept by his father which was usual. However, this measure turned Sanders, an impressive youth, against his pious father. His mother, Freedom Edgerton Sanders, had hoped her son would follow her brother Sidney and study law. Young Sanders attended an academy in Phelps, New York and earned a teaching degree. With a love for learning, he became a voracious reader...the Bible, Shakespeare, poetry, history, etc. At age twenty, he moved to Akron, Ohio to teach school and study law with his uncle. Much of his political aspects and motivations came from uncle Sidney.

Sanders was admitted to the Ohio State Bar in 1856. In October of 1858, he married a twenty-four year old he had met while teaching, Harriet Peck Fenn. She, like Sanders, had a Puritan ancestry from Massachusetts, was a woman of remarkable character and strength and an avid reader like Sanders. She was also a natural writer and a gifted painter. James, their first son, was born in July of 1859 and a second son Wilbur followed in August of 1861.

With the outbreak of the Civil War, Sanders volunteered in the Union Army and saw action in several fields including the Battle of Pittsburgh Landing. In August of 1862, he was forced to resign due to an illness provoked by his battle wounds. Upon his discharge, he returned to Akron. He carried his military rank into history and was often mentioned as "Colonel Sanders" in public life.

A LONG TRAIL...a hard ride

Also in the family trail party heading west was Sidney's wife Mary, their four children, Martha (Mattie), Wright, Sidney and Pauline, plus a niece Lucia Darling. In the Sanders group was Wilbur, his wife Harriet, their two sons James and Wilbur and Sanders' young nephew,

Henry Tilden. Almaretta, "Amerette" Geer, a maid to Mrs. Sanders accompanied the group and would prove to be most helpful on the coming trip.

The group left Akron by train to Chicago, then St. Louis and onto Omaha, Nebraska where they were outfitted with covered wagons, oxen and drivers, who also served as protection. Fully outfitted they began the arduous and hazardous trek across rugged country yet unknown to them. The Edgerton and Sanders wagon train would link with other wagons heading west and travel from Omaha through Nebraska, past Scotts Bluff and into what is now Wyoming. Just past Lander Cutoff, close to the present day western border of Wyoming, they turned north into the new Territory of Idaho and headed to the yet unknown Capitol. After crossing the central portion of Wyoming, the men and oxen faced the difficult task of climbing the precipitous slopes of the Continental Divide.

A telegraph operator they had talked to earlier from South Pass, a small town at the foot of the Wind River Mountains, rode up to the Edgerton train and told them he had finally received notice the Idaho Territory capitol would be located at Lewiston.

Edgerton originally appointed to the newly designated Capitol had a choice to make. The group heard of a rich gold strike to the north and Lewiston was still over two-hundred more rugged miles across both the steep Bitterroot Range and the Clearwater Range. With the weather turning colder, they chose to head for a closer gold mining town, *Bannack.* Splitting away from the other wagons, the four wagons of the Edgerton and Sanders group were destined to become an integral part of the richest gold rush eras of the country and a formidable part of the history of Montana.

Their ninety-three day trip from Omaha to Bannack was written into the records by Wilbur Sanders' wife Harriet, with a day-by-day recording of their experiences on the trail into rugged and unknown country. Following are some of the brief excerpts of Harriet Sanders' legendary journal:

"Omaha to Bannack: Summer 1863."

June 16, 1863; *"We all left the Herndon Hotel in Omaha in a large carriage, overtook our teams and went two and a half miles and camped, our first night in the prairies. Considering the conveniences, we thought we had a pretty good sleep."*

Tuesday, June 23; *"We have just heard of a battle fought yesterday between our troops and the Indians only twenty miles from here [sixteen miles up Loupe Fork of the Platte.] The Sioux beat the Pawnees and our* troops, and they have telegraphed for more of our men to come. I hope we shall have no trouble with Indians. Tonight we have camped only fifteen miles from the battleground, and the hills on the right are guarded by Indian scouts. The men have their guns all loaded and ready for a brush."

Sunday, June 28; *"Willie seemed rather feverish. I gave him a Dovers powder (Powder of ipecac and opium.)"*

Wednesday, July 1; *"We have been from home one month. Have had a pleasanter journey and better health than I expected. Saw in the distance three buffalo grazing, also ten beautiful antelope bounding over the plains but not near enough for a shot. Saw as many as fifty or sixty buffalo heads lying near the road."*

Sunday, July 5; *"I went to the top of a hill near our wagons about 200 feet high. There we had a fine view of the Platte Valley, the high bluffs on the opposite side of the river and the North and South Forks. We learned tonight that there are fifteen hundred Sioux camped for the night on an island five miles down the river from us. They are on their way to the reservation to fight the Pawnees."*

Tuesday, July 7; *"Last night we were all awakened by the loud cry of 'Stampede, stampede!' The men were up and out in no time and found that about forty of Creighton's cattle were within a few yards of our wagons. We camped early tonight on the banks of a tributary of the Platte to do a little washing. Whilst we were down at the water, we saw four warriors on horseback riding up to our camp, the first we had seen since Fort Kearney. After watching our preparations for supper, they motioned for some tobacco. The men gave them some...and bid them goodbye...but it was not easy getting rid of them."*

Wednesday, July 8; *"This morning we had breakfast ready for an early start, when lo, the poor Indians 'smelt a rat' and over they came on the run for something to eat. We gave them some meat, crackers, biscuit, and coffee, which they took, and seating themselves on the ground in a circle, ate their meal and behaved more mannerly than I expected to see an Indian."*

Friday July 10; *" This noon we were resting after dinner when...we were enveloped in a thick cloud of smoke...and the scent accompanying it inspired the belief the prairie was on fire. We yoked up our cattle and were soon on our way, leaving the smoke in our rear.... We decided that should the fire come in sight, we would drive to the river with all speed."*

Thursday, July 16; *"It was so cold last night that in addition to all the clothes I could muster, I put Mr. Sanders' overcoat on the bed. We (later) came to a grave bearing the inscription, 'Elwood Morris, aged 7 years. Died August 7, 1862.' We have passed a grave every day for a week past."*

Friday, July 24; *"Met some soldiers going to Julesburgh on the South Fork of the Platte. Wrote a line home and gave them to mail. They say there is no doubt the capital [of Idaho Territory] will be at Bannack City."*

Monday, August 3; *" This noon, just before we reached camp, we met with a bad accident, the first we have had since starting. Coming down a steep pitch, one of the wheels of Mr. Chipman's wagon...broke a number of spokes, and we are obliged to stop."*

Wilbur Sanders and some of the party had recalled seeing a broken wheel on the trail two or three days back. He started back on his horse to retrieve the needed spokes.

"After riding till darkness overtook him and he could see no signs of the trail, he spent the night in the mountains with only the horse for a companion. He could hear the wolves in the distance and momentarily expected they would attack him. He said it was the loneliest night he had ever experienced and the first time he had ever felt that he was lost. As soon as it was light, he succeeded in finding the trail and continued his search for the broken wheel, which he at last found.... Mr. Sanders came back bringing eight wheel spokes. It has taken all day to repair the damages and the men vote the wheel better than it was before it was broken."

Friday, August 7; *"We did not start till noon. I baked thirteen loaves of bread, which was no small job. Passed a flock of twelve wild geese, fired at them but did not hit any. After camping saw five antelope on a hill at a little distance...."*

Saturday, August 15; *"It was very cold last night. The water froze one-half inch thick. We shall have cold nights till we get a little down in the mountains. Yesterday when we were about ten miles this side of the South Pass Station, the telegraph operator overtook us to tell us that he had just received a dispatch from Salt Lake saying that the capital was located at Lewiston. We were all glad to hear it was at Lewiston, from what I hear, I think it will be far pleasanter and provisions will be cheaper than at Bannack."*

Tuesday, August 25; *"Passed two graves this A.M., the first we have seen in a number of weeks. One was in the loveliest of places. In a little grove there was a grave with a fence around it, a chair inside, and some double poppies on the grave, just in blossom. And a tree at the head of the grave with the lines, 'Elizabeth, wife of Thomas Paul, died in child bearing, July 27th, 1862.'"*

Wednesday, September 2; *"We overtook Creighton's train this morning of thirty-two wagons. He lost thirty cattle since starting and has five with him that can hardly crawl. This noon we came to the 'Bannack Cut-Off' and left all our company. They have 150 miles to Bannack and we about 400 miles to Lewiston."*

Friday, September 4; *" Hoped to reach Snake River, but met a man this P.M. who told us it was 20 miles from here."*

Saturday, September 5; *"Stopped at 3 P.M. within two miles of Snake River ferry. Mr. Sanders has gone on to the ferry to ascertain in regard to the route and distances to different points."*

Sunday, September 6; *"The express from Bannack to Salt Lake passed here today. We all wrote letters home. The weather is perfectly delightful. They tell us that we shall have good roads to Bannack, and we have decided to go that way instead of to the Boise mines. I shall cross the ferry tomorrow."* (Note: The "express" noted above carried Electa Bryan Plummer, leaving Henry Plummer who returned to Bannack.)

Monday, September 7; *"The Frenchman at the ferry charged so high to ferry us over that we went ten miles above to a ford, reached the ford about noon. There were two young men there, one from Ohio, who had been to the Boise mines and were on their way to Bannack."* *"It was by far the richest experience we have had. We made a good drive this afternoon followed by a half dozen Indians to get their supper."*

Sanders found a way to ford the river...but not without problems. The river was swift, pulling one wagon downstream. Sanders was able to stop the wagon, save the driver, and redirected them across the river. With water splashing onto the wagon box, occupants feared drowning. Sanders and several men, took the scared women and crying children across to safety by horseback. An Indian who rode up pulled Amerette Geer onto his horse and carried her across. When safely across, all had a sigh of relief at the experience.

Tuesday, September 8; *"Met some men with wagons going to Salt Lake, who said that the new mines just discovered not far from Bannack were by far the richest ever found yet."*

Saturday, September 12; *"We are only 100 miles from Bannack, where we expect to stop for a few days at least."*

Wednesday, September 16; *"Took our breakfast at noon, were all hungry. Made a drive of 20 miles, camped for dinner at the Red Bluffs 40 miles from Bannack. Three months today we left Omaha."*

Thursday, September 17; *"Came eight miles this morning and camped for the afternoon. We have had good feed and water for the cattle, and there is none this side of Bannack, which is thirteen miles. The weather is delightful. The air is so pure that we can see the moon all day."*

Friday, September 18; *"Started about 9 A.M. Reached Bannack City at 3 P.M."*

(Note: Above are only a small portion of the daily entries by Mrs. Harriet Sanders regarding the three-month trip from Omaha.) [2]

BANNACK...a new home.

Sanders acquainted himself with the small community and met many of the businessmen and shopkeepers. He soon met and became intimate friends with Frank Thompson, a businessman who had just opened a new shop with young Joseph Swift. Just days before Sanders arrived in Bannack, miner William Fairweather came to town to buy supplies. He and his group had discovered another rich gold strike just seventy miles east of Bannack. They named the area "Alder Gulch" after the surrounding trees. The young gold town was growing with a small population of miners, shopkeepers and support stores. When the Edgerton and Sanders families arrived there were no available houses. Young James Sanders, only four years old, consolidated the families' feelings about the new community with a bold remark, *"I fink Bangup is a humbug!"* [3]

Sanders searched for suitable living quarters for his family. Any log cabin would be an improvement over the wagons and tents they occupied over the past three months. He was able to find a large two room cabin owned by a merchant who lived in only half and willing to rent the other half.

When Mrs. Sanders viewed their "living" quarters she was not sure if her joy of having something solid over their heads outweighed her disappointment of the 18x20 foot single room with only a dirt floor. Two rooms were arranged by hanging muslin sheets and the owner agreed to have a wood floor installed. Her satisfaction came only when rugs and primitive wood furniture were arranged.

Mail to the new cabin in Bannack was limited, as they had planned on Lewiston as their new address. Each letter cost one dollar by both sender and receiver. The new Sanders family residence was located only feet from a cabin housing James and Martha Vail and their two children, who arrived just shortly before from the government farm at Sun River. Vails had purchased their cabin from Henry Plummer.

Sanders recalled seeing Plummer and his wife at the Snake River crossing in September. He soon learned Plummer's wife had left him for some unexplained reason to return to her family in Iowa. The Vail family proved to be friendly and sociable neighbors.

The thoughts of being in the midst of gold enthused Sanders. His legal knowledge would become more and more in demand. The influx of people and new found claims would augment the need for an attorney. However, with the incoming miners and shopkeepers would be a high percentage of "ne'er-do-wells" and drifters. This would also call upon Sanders' skills. [4]

Chapter Notes

Note 1. The above notes from Harriet Sanders Journal, Omaha to Bannack, Summer, 1863 are but a portion of the original notes taken. See *Biscuits and Badmen: The Sanders Story in Their Own Words.*

CHAPTER 9
THOMPSON meets CUTTHROATS
BEACHY dreams of AXE MURDER
Fall & Winter, 1863

Frank Thompson and partner Joseph Swift waited at Sun River for the arrival of the steamship which they thought had aboard the expected shipment of goods for their new store. When notified the ship had ran aground and passengers and goods had been unloaded at Cow Island, Swift traveled overland to arrange for the six tons of supplies to be transported by pack train to Bannack.

Thompson, at Sun River, decided to return to the store in Bannack and wait for Swift and the supplies to arrive. He rode back in a horse drawn, two wheel wagon he named the "go-devil."

THOMPSON...meets Doc

Arriving at Deer Lodge Camp from Sun River, Thompson stopped to buy supplies for the trip. The storekeeper warned him that traveling alone could be dangerous because of Indian problems along the trail. He also told Thompson about a group of riders, camped about a mile south, looking for someone to guide them to Bannack. Thompson met with the leaders of the group, Doc Howard and James Romaine. They appeared to Thompson to be educated and friendly.

Howard claimed to have studied at Yale Medical School. Romaine had worked in Marysville, California as a contractor and as a gambler, up the coast, in The Dalles. Howard informed Thompson one man in his group, Steve Marshland, had a "lame back," and was unable to ride. Marshland, unknown to Thompson, had been shot while stealing horses in Lewiston. Thompson offered Marshland to trade the "go-devil" wagon for Marshland's horse. Thompson felt, however, the group of twelve men from Lewiston, under Howard's command, seemed too well organized to be simply miners searching for gold...they had something else in mind. [1]

MAGRUDER...Elk City merchant

Frank Thompson rode south with the Howard group and soon met a slow moving pack train from Elk City, Idaho led by Lloyd Magruder. Magruder had several wagons loaded with mining supplies and goods he planned to sell in Bannack. Thompson, with a new store in Bannack, and his own load of supplies on its way from Cow Island, could have some competition...or a possible partner.

Magruder, a well-liked merchant in Elk City, was too trusting to be traveling alone in this "reign of terror"... as Thompson called it. When Magruder originally started out on his trip, Doc Howard, Jim Romaine, Chris Lowry, Bob Zachary and three other roughs headed out from Elk City in the opposite direction, toward Oregon, but stealthily doubled back to follow the Magruder train...a rich reward for robbers. After several days on the trail Howard's group was joined by an old, learned teamster and mountaineer, Billy Page.

At a crossing of the Big Hole River, the group heard of the new gold strike at Alder Gulch. However, both Magruder and Howard's group decided to stop at Bannack with Thompson for several days to refresh the horses and rest.

On the morning of the fifth day on the trail, Thompson walked into Bannack and met Sheriff Plummer. He told Plummer of the group he led to town and said some knew him and spoke well of him. Plummer replied with guarded concern, *"They speak well of me for they don't dare do otherwise."* Plummer continued, *"Thompson, those men are cutthroats and robbers! Hell will be to pay now! You need not associate with them any more than you choose."* Thompson questioned Plummer's concern, wondering how he knew of these..."cutthroats and robbers." [2]

CUTTHROATS...the leader

Doc Howard appeared educated, but it is doubtful he ever attended Yale Medical School. He got his medical education at the same school as Plummer...San Quentin Prison! At age twenty-eight Howard had been convicted of robbery and sent to prison for five years. He worked as trustee in the same infirmary and under the same physician that helped Plummer. (See chapter 3).

Howard's real name was David Renton. The Governor released him from San Quentin in August, 1858, about six months before Plummer entered the prison. The Governor, however, stipulated that Howard had to leave California and never return.

"DOC" HOWARD...an ominous "Shadow"

Magruder thought the new strike would bring a better return on the sale of his goods. He decided to go the extra miles east to Alder Gulch. Doc Howard and his group of "drifters" gladly offered to help him get there, set up the stock and sell it...Magruder gratefully agreed. It took about six weeks to sell off the goods to miners, grog shops and dry goods stores in the quickly growing area.

Magruder was happy for the help and to make such a good sale... about $24,000 in gold dust, greenbacks and coins, plus several mules he gained in trade. Magruder prepared his trip home through Bannack. Doc Howard now knew and concocted furtive plans regarding the rich booty Magruder had gained.

Four other men, including two young brothers, Horace and Robert Chalmers, from Missouri, agreed to unite and accompany Magruder. They made a brief stop in Bannack, where Howard again offered his men as "security" to Magruder for the remainder of his trip. Magruder wrote his wife to let her know he should arrive in Lewiston in about twelve days. The letter left Bannack two days before Magruder began his trip home. Magruder prepared his trip home from Alder Gulch through Bannack.

HILL BEACHY...bad dream

Meanwhile back in Lewiston, Hill Beachy, a good friend of Magruder, told his wife he had a bad dream...Chris Lowry would kill Magruder with an axe! Beachy's wife pooh-poohed the dream as nonsense, *"Don't tell that to anyone!"*

Beachy operated the Luna House, a regular stage-line stop in Lewiston. He was well aware of Lowry's past criminal history, but not all of it! Beachy knew the people in Lewiston and was well acquainted with law enforcement. He was unaware, however, that Lowry had escaped from San Quentin prison after serving only three years of a five year sentence for grand larceny.

Plummer and his gang knew of Doc Howard and had suspected an upcoming plot by him to plunder Magruder's rich rewards from Alder Gulch. While still in Bannack, Doc Howard proposed to Chris Lowry and Jim Romaine his dire plan to rob and kill Magruder and his four companions on the trail to Lewiston. They agreed to Howard's plan, but when asked to take part, Bob Zachary, as criminal as he was, declined.

Billy Page, the aged teamster from Oregon, was suspected by Howard to possibly resist his plan, not the robbery...but especially the killing. However, Howard needed Page, who had special knowledge of the backwoods trails. Howard decided not to disclose any proposed killing to Page until after they were on the trail to Lewiston, afraid he would pull out of his plan.

BITTERROOT VALLEY...cold

In early October, six days after leaving Bannack, Magruder's train had three more days to reach the cutoff to Lewiston. They had to cross through the high mountain passes in the Bitterroot Mountain Range, the Clearwater Range, then north to Lewiston. On the trail, with a cold chill in the high mountain wind, clouds overhead threatened snow. They rode into a valley with good pasture and water for their horses and mules. They hurriedly prepared camp before the storm.

Howard rode up the train of slow moving mules, alongside Page, and in a stern low voice said, *"Page, when we go into camp, tonight, drive the mules half a mile away, and remain with them until supper time. We are going to kill Magruder and his four friends. You can help dispose of the bodies when the work is done. As you value your own life, you will not breathe a word of this to any one."* Page was terrified. He never had blood on his hands...should he warn Magruder?...but would Magruder believe him? Howard developed a belied friendship with Magruder and gained his trust. Page had no choice...if he didn't obey Howard there would be one more body to dispose of...his!

At the campsite Howard met Page as he came in for supper, told him to retire after he ate and stay there until he was called. Page spread his blankets close to Phillips and prepared a bed, *"Not to sleep,"* he told later, *"but to await the course of events."*

He watched as Magruder and Lowry left to tend to the animals. Lowry picked up an axe on the way, saying he would, *"... build a fire."* The horses were quieted for the night and Doc Howard soon joined the men with a hot pot of coffee.

MOUNTAIN MASSACRE...no tombstones

After tending to the mules and horses, Magruder decided to relax with a smoke from his favorite pipe. He stooped over the warm fire to light his pipe when an axe, wielded by Chris Lowry, tore open his skull... confirming the dream of Hill Beachy...and the death of Lloyd Magruder! Magruder fell lifelessly into the fire. Howard rushed forward, grabbed the axe from Lowry and angrily dealt a savage final blow!

Howard and Lowry quietly returned to the main part of the camp. Page and Phillips were bedded on the ground. Phillips was asleep, but Page was wide awake!

Howard motioned to Romaine to follow...both carried axes. They walked past Page to the sleeping Chalmers brothers and simultaneously dealt deadly blows to both of them! Page heard the deathly strike of the axe, the groans, then silence...and he shuddered!

At the same moment, Romaine walked by Page, who wistfully looked up at him. Romaine whispered an order to Page, *"Lay still. Now you lay still!"* Romaine continued to Phillips, who was asleep, raised his axe and bludgeoned him! Phillips screamed! Again Page uncontrollably shuddered! Romaine dealt another killing blow to Phillips, and angrily shouted at his victim, *"You son-of-a-bitch, you shouldn't have come on this trip. I told you not to come!" I wish to Christ Bill Rhodes had come, I've wanted to kill that son-of-a-bitch for a long time!"* After his loud tantrum at Phillips' lifeless and bloody body, Romaine gasped and tried to catch his breath. He turned to Page and said, *"You're scared, you're shaking!"* He tried to console Page, *"Now don't be frightened."* After the slaughter Page had just witnessed, nothing could calm him. Charley Allen, chief packer for Magruder, anticipated snowfall during the night and had prepared a tent. He was inside the tent, asleep and did not hear the deadly commotion.

Doc Howard had discarded the bloody axe he used to kill Chalmers and picked up a shotgun. He quietly walked toward the front of Allen's tent. Afraid Phillip's screams would awaken Allen, Howard quickly pulled the tent flap open and recklessly shot Allen in the back of the head, blowing half of his skull into oblivion!

As he tried to appear calm, Howard walked down from Allen's tent and called out to Page, as he shuddered, *"That's right. Don't be frightened, Uncle Billy. All the dirty work is done!"*

BURIAL...none needed

The bloody bodies of the five victims were wrapped in blankets and thrown into a deep canyon for the wolves. The bloody clothes of the dead, their guns, saddles, everything not of value to the killers, were burned or buried.

When they left in the morning, the mules who followed after the group, were led into a nearby ravine and shot. All evidence of the massacre would be under deep, fresh snow before they left. All the gold dust and loot had been collected and put into spare canteens. Now, the killers' main concern was...escape!

When Magruder did not arrive in Lewiston as he stated in his letter to his wife, she began to worry...and Hill Beachy became deeply concerned. The four killers were planning to avoid Lewiston, but the swollen Snake and Clearwater Rivers cut off their planned route of escape. They had no choice but to enter town and catch the stage. They left their horses at a nearby ranch at the edge of town and walked to the stage station.

SADDLE REPAIR...tells a tale

On the night of October 18, 1863, at the Lewiston stage station in the Luna House, Beachy busily attended to the books. His ticket agent talked to a scruffy, bearded man who wanted to purchase four tickets on the stage to Walla Walla. He kept trying to cover his face with his coat collar and scarf. When asked for the names of the passengers, he hesitated, then gave names that sounded overly common and suspicious. This drew the attention of Beachy...he knew something was amiss. He was sure he recognized the man and looked again...Chris Lowry!

Before the stage left Beachy searched out and confided his suspicions to his friend, a Judge, and urged to have the four men arrested. The Judge laughed and said Beachy's suspicions were groundless. He told Beachy that Magruder may have gone to Salt Lake City, or had been delayed, before he started home.

After the four suspicious characters had boarded the stage and left, their horses and saddles were found. An Indian hostler, who worked for Magruder, recognized one of the saddles...it definitely belonged to Magruder! Beachy finally convinced the Judge of his suspicions and warrants were issued.

It would take stubborn perseverance by Beachy, Lloyd Magruder's close personal friend, to determine who the other killers were and to personally track them across the Northwest...from Walla Walla, Washington, into Oregon and finally to San Francisco, where they were arrested.

A RUEFUL PLOT...turns a page

Hill Beachy had all four suspicious characters extradited to Idaho Territory to face trial. He knew Howard, Lowry and Romaine would fight the charges, but felt Billy Page would be the most likely to confess. Beachy devised a rueful plot: A surreptitious hanging of Page by a "rogue band" of Vigilantes...and the hanging of the other three would be "planned" before any trial could take place.

Beachy set the stage. He had a room set up next to the interrogation room of the killers...where four ropes with a hangman's noose were plainly visible. The ruse scared Page and convinced him, a victim of circumstance, to give damning evidence against his cohorts. Page would later reveal to the courts the actual site in the Bitterroot Mountains where the massacre took place. Remains of Magruder and his friends were found and properly interred by their families.

Doc Howard, Jim Romaine and Chris Lowry were tried by a jury and convicted of murder. After the three heard the jury's report, Judge Samuel Parks ordered them to stand and he read a lengthy and firm closing statement on their guilt. His poignant declaration stated; *"Another thing your (past) history illustrates:...It is that there is no security to any man in the commission of such crimes, no matter how wild or remote the place of commission. You vainly thought by murder of all your fellow travelers you secured silence and safety. You burned the blood of Magruder, that it might not reveal your guilt; but like the blood of Abel it cried to God against you... and the cry was heard and answered...!"*

Judge Parks then announced, on March 4, 1864, the three would be hanged by the neck until dead. Page, for his testimony, was turned over to the court and released...but, his reprieve was short! He was shot and killed Christmas day, 1866, by a man he had once before beat up in a barroom fight. The remainder of the stolen money, approximately $17,000, was returned to Magruder's wife. Hill Beachy served in various law enforcement positions until he retired to San Francisco where he died in 1875. [3][4][5]

Chapter Synopsis

This bloody murder and robbery of five hard working, law-abiding men in the ruthless gold camps of early-day Montana gives a brief insight of the players involved and meant to show just how dangerous the gold camps of the 1860's could be.

As an "elected sheriff," when Henry Plummer stated, "...those men are cutthroats and robbers!"...he knew the villainous motives of Doc Howard would come to no good for Magruder! Plummer had the duty to warn Magruder, just as he warned Frank Thompson earlier. Not doing so, made Sheriff Plummer and any of his gang members who knew Doc Howard and his accomplices...as guilty as the actual killers!

To Colonel Sanders, a new arrival to the Territory, this horrific episode of criminal behavior gave a him a terribly bold picture of the environment he and his family would be living in.

Chapter Notes

Note 1. For a more detailed reading of the Magruder murders and Hill Beachy's struggle to bring justice to the killers see Chapters XXXII and XXXIII of Nathaniel P. Langford's *Vigilante Days and Ways*, and Ladd Hamilton's *This Bloody Deed*.

Note 2. Chris Lowry was originally from Pennsylvania and had worked on the Mullan Expedition as a blacksmith. (Lowry's name as some family members use it has also been spelled: Lowerey, Lowery and Lower. The latter had been used in court records.)

Note 3. It was written by Dimsdale in his book, *Vigilantes of Montana*, first published in 1867, the plot to kill Magruder and rob his rewards from Alder Gulch sales was devised by Plummer's right hand man, Cyrus Skinner. This is deemed unlikely. It is believed the plotter was Doc Howard... and began in Elk City, Idaho when Howard's cohorts devised the plan, to head west to Oregon, to allay any suspicion of their following Magruder.

Robbers attack Gold Stage.

CHAPTER 10
BUMMER DAN & SOUTHMAYD ROBBERIES
Late Fall, Early Winter, 1863

Frank Thompson had set up a new store in Bannack and waited for young Swift to arrive with goods from Fort Benton. When Swift arrived, Thompson found he must pay $4,700 for the transportation of the supplies to Bannack...more than he paid for the goods.

SUSPICIONS...growing

Henry Plummer gave Thompson advice, or a warning, to stack heavy, bulky boxes toward the front of his new store. Thompson wondered why...was it to protect from stray gunfire? Could it be Plummer anticipated a fray with Doc Howard...which could possibly lead to a shooting?

In *"A Tenderfoot in Montana"* by Frank Thompson, the following excerpt is noted; *"After her (Electa) departure robberies became more and more frequent. Plummer, being my fellow boarder at Mrs. Vail's, I knew of all his absences and noticed, as my suspicions arose, that all big holdups and robberies happened when he was away from home. I recalled his warning when I told him of Doc Howard's arrival, and with what certainty he spoke of the future operation of the roughs. I became certain that he knew of the plans of the road agents before they were carried into execution. He was also the acknowledged owner of the Rattlesnake Ranch located about fifteen miles from Bannack, which harbored a notorious lot of scoundrels."* [1]

Thompson, close to Plummer, noted the suspicious acts of this devious character and was open-minded enough to understand them for what they were...criminal! Thompson suspected Plummer was aware of the robberies before they were carried out. Could he possibly have planned them?

Others believed deeply in this suspicion, such as Deer Lodge cattleman Conrad Kohrs, as well as mining entrepreneur Sam Hauser. Kohrs in his visits to Bannack and Alder Gulch consistently avoided the customary stage route past the Rattlesnake ranch.

Nathaniel Langford, member of the Union League, told Hauser the League's choice for Deputy Marshal of Idaho Territory was Plummer. Hauser, a prominent citizen, had serious apprehensions regarding Plummer. He wildly stated, *" ... the sheriff is a dangerous man!"* and continued, *"...possibly involved with the Dillingham murder!"*

Langford errantly discussed with Plummer the points Hauser made. Plummer was furious, *"Langford, you'll be sorry for this before the matter ends. I've always been your friend, but from this time on, I'm your enemy. And I say this, I mean in more ways than one!"* [2]

BUMMER DAN...takes a walk

Meanwhile, Plummer's road agents were busy...the robberies continued. Dan McFadden was commonly known in Virginia City as "Bummer Dan," because of his ingrown ability to beg...for meals, for drinks, even for a place to sleep. McFadden spent time as an aide to officers in the Union Army, a position which was tagged with the moniker, "Bummer." His ability to gain official favors in the army carried over into his life in the gold fields. However, he used other abilities to work his gold claim in the Dakota Lode, possibly the richest lode in the gulch. He "bummed" and labored hard enough to gain a stash of gold worth enough to make him decide to return to the States with his wealth.

Well aware of the possibility of losing his fortune to robbers on the road, McFadden planned to sneak out of town on foot and catch the stage along the way. After leaving Virginia City, the stage arrived at the first stop at the Stinking Water (Ruby) River. The stage driver waited for the hands to find fresh horses. When the stage reached the second stop at the Dempsey Ranch, Bummer Dan, wet and cold after walking through a snow squall, waited to board. Due to the storm the stage had not reached the Rattlesnake Ranch until late evening, the last stop before Bannack.

The ranch, with genial hosts Bill Bunton and Frank Parish, had plenty of booze and a good cook in the person of "Red" Yeager. The hospitality of the night gave plenty of chance for Bunton to observe the passengers and take note of any gold they may carry.

When time came for the stage to leave in the morning the replacement horses were nowhere to be found. They had to rehitch the tired team from the night before. At the last minute Bunton decided to join the stage and climbed into the seat with the driver. After a short time on the road he decided to ride with McFadden and climbed down into the coach.

DAN'S PLAN...foiled

Only moments later two masked men riding horses, hooded with blankets, rode up and stopped the stage. Aiming shotguns at the driver they told everyone to get out. The gunmen seemed to be concerned mainly with McFadden. They told driver Rumsey to take McFadden's gun and collect his pouches of gold dust. McFadden gave up two small pouches of dust from his coat pocket. One gunman quickly cursed McFadden and threatened to shoot him for hiding more gold. Bummer Dan envisioned his work, his gold, all would be lost. He slowly took off his coat and unstrapped a large pouch of gold dust hidden in his pants. Concerned, he wondered how the robbers knew about his hidden gold. The gunmen sternly warned passengers not to tell anyone about the robbery...and they rode off with all of Bummer Dan's savings.

Granville Stuart in October, 1863, wrote in his diary, *"Unusual excitement in town today."* He reported, *"' Bummer Dan' McFadden lost $2,500 ...in a highway robbery...."* Passengers noted Bill Bunton's unusual display of panic during the hold-up. He begged, *"For God's sake don't shoot. Take what I have, but don't kill me."* For those who knew Bunton, he acted strangely out of character. Stuart's diary also noted something strange, *"... Sheriff Plummer did not seem eager to catch the bad guys."*

This appeared as a change in the pattern of random robberies that had been reported previously. It was a planned holdup targeting McFadden. Bunton rode the stage because he already knew of McFadden's riches. He had seen the pouch of gold the night before and told his cohorts of Mc Fadden's hidden cache. Despite "Bummer Dan's" attempt to deceive the gang of his large horde of gold, he could not avoid being robbed! The two masked robbers were unknown to McFadden, but suspected to be good friends of Bunton. [3]

MASKED MEN...horses too

When robbers with masks stopped their proposed targets, they also had "masks" for their horses. They could often be recognized by distinct markings or tack...bridles, saddles or stirrups. The robbers' horses were "masked" with blue-green blankets from their head to their tail, which covered most of their distinct markings or color. If seen later, robbers could be recognized by what they wore, boots or spurs. Their horses were corralled at local ranches and seen by many people and could also be recognized by someone who had been robbed. Plummer had gang-members in the area between Bannack and Virginia City who stayed at his Rattlesnake Ranch, at Dempsey's, and other ranches along the trail, and they and their horses could easily be recognized.

SOUTHMAYD...no help from the law

In late November, 1863, Leroy Southmayd arranged passage on the A. J. Oliver & Co. stage from Alder Gulch, through Bannack to Salt Lake City. He traveled with two other passengers, Captain Moore and a second driver named Billy. As they waited to board they noticed a bedraggled, time-worn miner "Tex" Crowell. He drew their suspicions. It would surely disturb anyone to have Crowell around, especially when carrying gold dust.

At their first stop at Laurin's ranch on the Stinking Water River, their suspicions grew when they saw George Ives. Ives was a handsome rancher and an excellent horseman, but, when intoxicated, he became dangerously obnoxious. He was unpredictable, sober or drunk! Southmayd avoided any conversation with Ives, but heard him say he would meet with "Tex."

The stage continued past the ranch without problems and onto Beaverhead Rock station where Southmayd spent a nervous night. Ives, while still at Cold Springs ranch, met with two other road agents, Whiskey Bill Graves and Bob Zachary, and they proceeded to ride past Beaverhead Rock and down the trail...to hide and wait for the stage.

The next day the stage was stopped on the trail to Bannack by the three masked road agents with shotguns. Their horses were covered by the blue-green blankets. Driver Tom Caldwell stopped the coach and Ives ordered everybody out. He told Zachary to get down, collect their guns and search everyone for gold. Zachary was nervous, trembling noticeably, as he searched Southmayd. However, Southmayd was more concerned with who the robbers were...he strained to see as much as he could.

When the gun of the second driver was taken, Ives asked if it was loaded. Billy said it was not and Ives told Zachary to give it back. The robbers collected over $400 in gold dust from Southmayd, $100 from Captain Moore, who complained bitterly, and several small pouches of gold from driver Caldwell. They also searched the mail sack for any letters with gold. Ives felt they had found everything and told the passengers to *"Get up, and skedaddle."* As he climbed onto the stage, Southmayd turned to get a better look at the robbers. Ives saw him and yelled, *"If you don't mind your own business, I'll shoot the top of your head off."*

QUESTIONING...begins

Sheriff Plummer met the stage at Bannack and asked if the stage had been robbed and did anyone recognize any of the robbers. Southmayd was about to tell Plummer the details when, Dr. Gaylord Bissell, standing nearby, abruptly pulled Southmayd aside and warned, *"...do not tell Plummer anything!"* Bissell was among those who did not trust the Sheriff. Southmayd ignored Bissell's warning and turned to face Plummer.

Before he could say a word, Plummer quickly stated he thought he knew the robbers. *"Who?"* Southmayd blurted. Plummer started to answer...again Southmayd boldly interrupted, *"George Ives was one of them..."* and he hurriedly continued, *"I know...and the others were Whiskey Bill and Bob Zachary... and I'll live to see them hanged!"*

After Plummer left, Dr. Bissell cautioned Southmayd, that what he told Plummer about the robbers would put his life in danger. *"Leroy,"* he said, *"your life is not worth a cent!"* Standing nearby George Crisman added, *"They'll kill you sure!"*

KNOWLEDGE...is dangerous

Southmayd stayed in Bannack and the next day returned to Alder gulch by stage with Tom Caldwell. Both were alarmed to find Plummer's deputies, Ned Ray and Buck Stinson on the coach. Most of the trip was uneventful until they came to Cold Spring station, where Whiskey Bill and Bob Zachary stood with another rumored road agent, Aleck Carter. All had guns and intently watched the stage. Unexpectedly Stinson called out from the coach, *"Ho! You damned road agents."* Southmayd glanced at Caldwell. He didn't know who to fear the most, the deputies inside the coach...or the road agents!

When Plummer's deputies made no attempt to arrest anyone, Southmayd feared what would surely happen. He told Caldwell, *"Tom, we're done for!"* However, the trio lowered their guns and went back into the station house.

Fresh horses were hitched to the stage, everyone reboarded and continued towards Alder Gulch. However, before anyone could get settled, the trio from the station rode up beside the coach and called out, *"Halt!"* Southmayd and Caldwell cocked their guns and leveled them at the horsemen. Aleck Carter threw up his hands and in a halting gesture, daringly said, *"We only want you to take a drink. But you can shoot and be damned if you want to!"* He handed a bottle of whiskey to Caldwell and Southmayd. They merely touched the bottle to theirs lips, with the thought it may be poisoned. The three men shouted farewell and rode off...laughing.

Stinson and Ray alternated singing loudly on the coach, all the way into Alder Gulch...a signal for other road agents to stay away, not to bother the stage. [4] [5]

The day following the hold-up, George Ives entered a lavish bar in Virginia City, got drunk and started to boast openly about robbing Caldwell. He boldly told another driver of the same stage company, *"I am the Bamboo chief that committed that robbery."* The driver asked, *"Don't you believe Caldwell knows it?"* *"Certainly he knows it,"* Ives replied with stern indifference, *"He recognized me at once."* The driver knew it was Ives' intent to kill Caldwell...as soon as he had the chance. [6] [7]

Chapter Notes

Note 1. Leroy Southmayd, a Mason, was buried in the Virginia City cemetery in May, 1883. He did live..."to see them hanged."...as he had stated! It is believed Southmayd, because of his forthright declaration to Plummer, had close connections with the Vigilance Committee and had some knowledge of the Vigilantes' preparations for ending the holdups and murders.

Note 2. Unlike Wild West movies of today, not all citizens carried personal firearms. The miners, storekeepers and general citizens seldom carried a pistol, and if so, it was more than likely carried in their belt or pocket.

CHAPTER 11
HAUSER and LANGFORD
MOODY WAGON TRAIN ROBBERY
Late Summer to Midwinter, 1863

HAUSER and LANGFORD...to Salt Lake City

It was early November, 1863, as Samuel Hauser boarded the Alder Gulch stage to go to Bannack. He planned to meet Nathaniel Langford and they would continue to Salt Lake City with a Mormon wagon train. Dance & Stuart, merchants in Virginia City, asked Hauser to deliver $14,000 in gold dust to their creditors in Salt Lake. Hauser boarded the stage in Alder Gulch and was surprised he would have company... Henry Plummer. He became nervous with so much gold. When the stage arrived in Bannack, without any problems, Langford was also surprised to see Plummer.

Knowing Plummer was now aware of the amount of gold they would carry, Hauser boldly gave the pouch to him, asking to hold it for safe keeping, since they would leave the next day. Plummer agreed, saying he would keep it in his office in Bannack. This was a bold move on Hauser's part, which caught both Plummer and Langford off guard. What could Plummer do? There were witnesses to his taking possession of the gold. He returned the gold to Langford the next day and also presented Hauser with a bright red scarf... *"to keep you warm on the trip."* Wearing the scarf was a signal to Plummer's road agents there was bounty on board and who would have it.

LANGFORD PREPARES...a deadly shot

Langford cleaned his gun in preparation for their planned trip, loading both barrels of his shotgun with twelve pistol balls...a deadly weapon against any robbers. Langford and Hauser had planned to meet the Mormon wagon train in the evening at Horse Prairie south of Bannack and continue together onto Salt Lake City the next day. However, they were late leaving town...which put a hitch in their schedule.

When Langford and Hauser finally did meet with the Mormons at their camp, Hauser bunked in one of the wagons while Langford slept on the ground near the campfire under a thick buffalo robe.

Meanwhile back at Bannack, Plummer prepared to spread his "alibi." He would claim he had to leave town shortly...on business. He had been "asked" to appraise a recently discovered silver lode out of town. This was his excuse when he knew there was gold being carried by stage in or out of Bannack. He would then ride in the opposite direction of the planned robbery so he could claim to be, *"...no where near the area."*

However, Plummer made a second excuse to other people at the Goodrich Hotel. His helper at the Rattlesnake ranch, Frank Parish, was sick and he feared Parish might pass away and his Indian wife would steal all his horses and take them to an Indian camp near West Lemhi. He had to make sure his horses would not be stolen.

SANDERS...follows Plummer

Wilbur F. Sanders and Sidney Edgerton were interested in any rich strikes they could invest in. They thought Plummer had left to appraise a new claim north of town. Sanders decided, hopefully, to follow Plummer. He borrowed a mule to ride to the ranch, but the aged mule was stubborn...and had to be pulled most of the way while Sanders walked. When he arrived at the Rattlesnake Ranch, Red Yeager told him Plummer was not there. This puzzled Sanders. Tired and hungry from pulling the mule, he asked for something to eat. Red fixed some dried beef and Sanders bedded down and fell asleep.

About midnight Jack Gallagher, a deputy for Plummer, burst into the ranch house. He had been riding from Bannack in the night and had lost his way. He also was looking for Plummer, but needed and demanded a fresh horse. Awakened, Sanders asked Gallagher if he knew where Plummer was...which infuriated Gallagher. He pulled his pistol, pointed it at Sanders and threatened to shoot him. Gallagher looked at Yeager and hollered, *"Who is this...why is he asking about Plummer?"*

Sanders distracted Gallagher, reached Yeager's shotgun behind the bar, pointed it at Gallagher and told him if there was any shooting to be done he would have the first shot. At that point Yeager intervened and calmed Gallagher down.

Reluctantly, Gallagher apologized and asked Sanders to drink with him. Red Yeager brought out some more beef and drinks and everyone relaxed. Shortly, Yeager and Gallagher went to the stable and exchanged Gallagher's horse for one of the stage line horses and Gallagher left.

Tired, they all settled down around the fireplace. Before anyone got to sleep, Gallagher pushed through the door again...he was still lost. Yeager put more wood on the fire and Gallagher, agitated but tired, spread his bedroll and everyone went to sleep.

Meanwhile, Plummer had left Bannack and headed north, as if to go to the Rattlesnake ranch alone. Instead, just out of town, he met three cohorts and all rode south to Horse Prairie. They planned to rob Langford and Hauser of their large cache of gold.

TILDEN...bumps into Plummer

Henry Tilden, nephew of Colonel Sanders, had been sent earlier that morning to search for stray cattle in Horse Prairie, a lush grazing meadow south and west of town. Riding several miles during the day, he found some of the cows, returned them to a nearby corral and had started back to Bannack. The evening sky was clear and cold with dim moonlight.

It was just turning dusk when Plummer and partners crested a bluff and were startled by an unexpected lone rider...Tilden. They hurriedly pulled their kerchiefs up, over their faces and pointed guns at him, told him to get off his horse...and put up his hands. The masked riders searched Tilden, finding only a couple of dollars, they cursed and told him to have more money next time or he would be shot!...and his body left for the wolves!...but this time, they would let him go.

Tilden scared, but glad to be still alive, climbed on his horse and quickly rode off. Close to town, his horse stepped into a ditch and spilled him onto the ground. Dazed, he gained his senses and stumbled to Sanders' cabin in Yankee Flats and told Sanders' wife what had happened. Still shivering from the cold he told her of his being robbed and gasped, *"I know one of the robbers. It was Henry Plummer!"* She quickly took her nephew to Edgerton's cabin to repeat his threatening experience.

LANGFORD...spooks robbers

After his unexpected meeting with Tilden, Plummer wondered where Langford, his prime interest, might be. He decided he had better find out. Hastily he rode back to town and learned Langford had already left to meet the Mormon freighters. It was near dusk and knowing he had little time left, Plummer hurriedly returned to Horse Prairie to rejoin his partners. [1]

At the Mormon Camp in Horse Prairie, Langford was asleep close to a dying fire when something unusual woke him. He stumbled from his bed and tended to the fire. In the darkness he heard voices near the camp. Cautiously he walked towards a dry creek bed and saw three masked men, with a fourth close-by holding several horses. Hearing

Langford in the bushes, the robbers thought they had been discovered. Their unexpected meeting with Tilden earlier made them decide their, as yet unknown, identity was worth more than Hauser's gold. The masked intruders quickly mounted their horses and rode back to Bannack. Langford and Hauser made the trip to Salt Lake City with the gold and without any further disturbances.

The next morning friends of Sanders came for him at the Rattlesnake Ranch. After Tilden's incident at Horse Prairie the night before, they worried about his safety. Sanders and his two friends rode back to Bannack. [2]

TILDEN'S TALE...questioned

After Colonel Sanders arrived home from his unrewarding trip, young Tilden repeated his tale of the frightening holdup.

Sanders questioned if the young boy had been able to actually recognize Plummer. Tilden was of undoubted integrity...he defiantly maintained his identification. Due to his crippled arm from the Crawford shooting, Tilden had easily recognized it was Plummer who shoved the pistol in his face...by the awkward way he handled his gun...left handed! Sanders warned Tilden he could be killed if he told anyone.

Some still doubted Tilden's story. Plummer was the Sheriff...and thought to be quite cordial! Tilden also added he recognized the red lining of Plummer's favorite black longcoat. To those who doubted Tilden and knew of Plummer's unique coat, it proved to be far more convincing.

Later, as written by Langford, he believed the four men discouraged from the attempted robbery at Horse Prarie were Sheriff Plummer, Buck Stinson, Ned Ray and George Ives. While still in Salt Lake City, Langford and Hauser were questioned about other missing people... known to have left Bannack weeks before...but never arrived. [3]

MOODY WAGON TRAIN ROBBERY...against all odds

Early December, 1863, less then a week after Plummer's bungled robbery in Horse Prairie, a wagon train left Virginia City with several merchants. Led by Milton Moody, the train carried trailblazer John Bozeman plus eight merchants, who carried $80,000 in gold dust for their Salt Lake creditors. Moody had planned a shortcut at the Red Rock cutoff, which would take them south of the gold strike at Bannack.

One merchant on the train, John McCormick, had befriended George Ives, and mentioned to him, unintentionally, about the planned trip. Ives cautioned him to stay alert during the trip, to watch for foul play until he crossed the Divide north of the Snake River.

Steve Marshland and "Dutch John" Wagner, who came into Bannack earlier, were both former members of "Doc" Howard's infamous group. They indiscreetly followed the train with foul intentions and expectations of reaping large rewards.

The train stopped at Blacktail Deer Canyon to prepare for dinner and a rest. Wagner had tried to convince Marshland it would be easier to surprise the drivers when they stopped to eat...Marshland disagreed, he felt they should wait.

Another chance soon came up, but as they approached, the drivers of the train spotted riders in the distance and cautiously armed themselves. Knowing they faced a shootout, Wagner and Marshland decided they change tactics. They approached the train openly, unmasked and boldly inquired about *"...some lost horses?"* The pair warily noted the fire-power they faced in a possible shootout...and rode off!

Finally, two days later, after following the train unnoticed, Marshland and Wagner had their chance. Four merchants of the train rode ahead and found a campsite for the night. Moody and Melancton Forbes, watched over a sick man in one of the wagons. A fourth man remained with the train. The pair of thieves took the opportunity and rode in, both carried double-barreled shotguns. Wagner guarded everyone while Marshland searched the wagons for guns and money. Nervous while he searched the baggage, he missed several canteens...loaded with gold dust. He also missed money in Moody's shirt pocket and a gun hidden in his boot!

Marshland found $1,500 in greenbacks in the first wagon, but as he nervously climbed into the third wagon, Forbes, who silently watched Marshland...shot him in the chest!   Wagner returned fire into the wagon, but his horse suddenly reared, sending his shot wild. Moody pulled the hidden pistol from his boot and fired at Wagner...hitting him in the shoulder. Wagner rode off and left Marshland on the ground, holding his bloody chest in pain. He struggled to his feet, stumbled into the thicket and escaped.

When the four merchants rejoined the group at a new campsite, Moody and several men returned to search for the wounded robbers. They recovered Marshland's horse and the $1,500 in greenbacks...but no robbers. [4]

HOWIE and FEATHERSTUN...capture Wagner

The Moody wagon train continued south and met Neil Howie, a past sheriff in Colorado with his partner John Featherstun, heading north to Bannack. They were told of the robbery attempt and given a description of the two thieves. Meanwhile Wagner, with a bullet in his shoulder, struggled into the hills. He froze his hands in the cold December weather, but finally risked going into a ranch in Horse Prarie.

Howie and Featherstun later happened to stop at the same ranch, recognized Wagner and arrested him. They took him to the Sears Hotel in Bannack. Featherstun remained to guard Wagner while Howie left to seek help. Several unknown men came to the hotel, confronted Featherstun and took Wagner as their prisoner. Featherstun, helpless to resist, had not known they were Vigilantes who had gathered in force in Bannack for a different reason. Several Vigilantes interrogated Wagner to gain knowledge about Plummer's possible connection to the Moody wagon train robbery. He did not confess to any Plummer involvement, but on January 11, 1864, Dutch John Wagner was hanged from the rafters of a small shop in Bannack. Two frozen bodies still remained in the building from an earlier hanging by the Vigilantes.

Marshland would later be found by the Bannack Vigilantes in a desolate cabin in the Big Hole Valley, half frozen with gangrene in both his legs and feet. His chest wound gave evidence he had taken part in the failed Moody wagon train robbery. He told the Vigilante search team had come within a few feet of him. On January 16, 1864, Steve Marshland would be hanged at a cabin in the Big Hole Valley. [5]

NEIL HOWIE TRIVIA...Plummer tries recruiting

Neil Howie, a former lawman, had a rough time making a living at the Bannack mines when Henry Plummer approached him stating,

"Neil, this is a hard way to get a living."

"I know it." replied Howie.

"I can tell you an easier way." suggested Plummer.

"I'd like to know it." queried Howie.

"There are plenty of men making money in this country," Plummer said, *"and we are entitled to a share of it."* Howie was not sure of Plummer's meaning, saying nothing.

"Come with me," Plummer asked, *"and you'll have all you want"*

Recognizing Plummer's intent, Howie replied, *"You've picked the wrong man."*

"All right." Plummer cooly replied, *"I suppose you know enough to keep your mouth shut!"*

Plummer had fallen short of "eyes and ears" for his gang and needed a few more "good" men. He approached Howie in the fall of 1863. Howie recalled what had happened to Dillingham, Plummer's former deputy. Plummer's recruiting attempt failed! [6]

Chapter Notes

Note 1. Henry Plummer, the robber chief was apparently careless, or inept, at planning. He sent only two men to rob a gold-laden wagon train...guarded by eight men. He had sent four men on an earlier robbery...but results were still the same...he gained nothing.

Note 2. Going back to the Tilden incident, it could be surmised that Tilden actually surprised Plummer and his three cohorts by accident, while they were really looking for Langford, Hauser and the rich Mormon wagon train. The same night, Plummer would find his target at camp and be surprised again...and foiled again! Thanks to Tilden's lonely job in Horse Prairie and Langford's delays in town, there was a fault in Plummer's planning and it paid off...but not for the road agents! This ineptitude may be coming from, as Frank Thompson noted, "more roughs in the area." With no control over others by Plummer, he had to think about his own spies, road agents and robberies. Whatever the cause, the local merchants and miners were becoming distraught over the constant robberies and killings. Why wasn't the Sheriff doing anything about it? Suspicions about "Sheriff" Henry Plummer mounted.

CHAPTER 12
SANDERS prosecutes FIRST TRIAL
Mid-December, 1863

OLD MAN CLARK...investigates

William "Old Man" Clark, of Burchey & Clark Store in Virginia City, awaited the return of his young employee Nicholas Tbalt. He had been gone for several days. Tbalt owned two good mules Clark wanted to buy. He had them pastured at "Long John's," a nearby ranch. Clark had already given Tbalt gold dust to pay for the mules. When he did not return Clark became worried. Tbalt was a hard working, well liked young man in the community, who Clark trusted. He asked a couple of friends to go up the Stinking Water River with him to look for Tbalt.

"X" Beidler agreed with Clark that something was amiss, but was unable to to go with him. William "Bill" Herron knew Tbalt and agreed to accompany Clark. Herron knew and had ridden, "Black Bess," the same mule Tbalt rode to "Long John's" ranch. Clark and Herron prepared their horses and bedrolls. Both decided to carry a pistol, hoping that would be sufficient...but not needed.

They reached Dempsy's Ranch to find several men working to load some freight wagons. One of the men, George Ives, who knew Clark was looking for Tbalt, arrogantly stepped up to Clark and questioned, *"Don't you think that Dutchman of yours has skipped to Salt Lake and taken the mules with him?"* Clark stared at Ives and sternly replied, *"That Dutchman is an honest man and some of you damned road agents have killed him...and I will avenge him!"*

Ives angrily stepped back and pulled his gun from his belt! Sensing trouble, Clark started for his gun, but "Whiskey Bill" Graves pushed between them and stopped a certain shootout. Bill Herron pulled Clark aside and calmed him down. After talking, Clark and Herron mounted and rode off towards Long John's ranch. Both nervously watched Ives and Whiskey Bill as they followed.

A short ride down the trail, Herron noticed a dark spot along the creek-side and they stopped. It had since snowed but the ensuing wind had blown the ground clear and showed a distinct splatter of blood. Clark looked, but saw no visible tracks in the area and assumed someone could have recently shot a deer.

Clark and Herron remounted and again spotted the same two men riding about a half mile ahead of them, also headed towards Long John's ranch. They reached the ranch and talked to George Hilderman, a ranch hand. He told Clark a Dutchman from Alder Gulch, riding a black mule, came and got two other mules. He paid for pasturing them and left about a week ago. Clark disgustedly mentioned to Herron that he felt they were at the trails' end of clues. Herron agreed...they stopped the search and headed home.

Stopping at Dempsey's again, they noticed two horses hitched outside, well lathered from a hard ride. Two shotguns were sheathed on the horses saddles. They thought surely Ives and Graves were inside. When they entered, Ives came up and sarcastically asked Clark if he had, *"... found the Dutchman?"* Clark angrily replied, *"I guess you know where that Dutchman is!"* Ives walked away and both Clark and Herron left Dempsy's. They rode off towards Pete Daley's ranch with hopes they would not encounter any further trouble.

CLARK...fighting mad

Clark proposed they stop at Daley's ranch for dinner. Herron agreed...he had seen enough excitement. He was hungrier than scared. Before they had been served, Ives and Whiskey Bill walked in, both carrying shotguns. Herron quickly persuaded Clark they had better leave...without eating...he was sure they were about to be killed. They hurriedly rode off, but saw the pair following them. Clark suggested they take a fork in the road and a seldom used trail into town. It could throw the road agents ahead of them...it worked! When Clark and Herron rode into Nevada City, Ives and Graves were already there, but they were unable to do any killing...without witnesses.

William Clark, suspected the worst for Tbalt and said, *"Those road agents have killed Nick, and I'll tell you what I propose to do. I helped organize the Vigilance committee in California and I'm going to do the same here. I'll make it hot for them before I die!"* "Old Man" Clark soon heard the news about young Tbalt...and would seek revenge! [1]

HUNTING...no luck, no help

It was a cold morning for hunting and William Palmer was not having any luck. As he rode along the banks of the Stinking Water River north of Alder Gulch, a grouse suddenly flew up in front of him. Surprised, he had little chance of hitting the bird...but fired anyway. The bird fluttered and fell into the brush. Hastening after the bird, Palmer stopped suddenly and shuddered at what he found hidden in the brush...a body! The young man had been shot in the head...with rope burns around his neck. The corpse still had clumps of brush in his clenched, frozen hands. This was not an accident! Palmer hurried to a nearby hut where he met two men, told them what he found, and asked for help getting the body into his wagon...they refused.

"Long John" Franck and George Hilderman worked at the ranch but appeared too afraid to become involved. Palmer thought it strange, these two bedraggled men would not help...they seemed to shy away from something they already knew about.

Puzzled, he left, and without help, was able to get the body into his wagon and rode into Nevada City. When Palmer arrived in town with the body...it was recognized to be the missing Nicholas Tbalt. A large crowd circled the wagon. In the pants pockets of the frozen body they found a favorite pocketknife known to belong to Tbalt...but no gold.

Robbery was added to murder...and "Long John" Franck and George Hilderman were the main suspects...but when Clark told about his experiences with George Ives, his name was added, and led the list of suspected culprits. The burn marks on Tbalt's neck and the brush in his frozen hands, indicated he suffered monstrous treatment, ending in his odious shooting. This angered Clark and many Alder Gulch residents who knew Ives had been involved in similar deadly actions, but showed no fear of reprisal, or a hint of remorse!

POSSE FORMED...the first

"Old Man" Clark, disgusted with all the ugly killings in the area, suggested to James "Cap" Williams they form a posse to arrest the suspected killers of Tbalt. Williams offered to supply horses from his ranch with enough saddles and equipment for the posse. About twenty men volunteered and urged Williams to ride with them. He had not planned to go, but reluctantly agreed to ride with them. Among others in the posse were George Burtschy, William Palmer, John "X" Biedler and Elk Morse.

They set out late on a cold December evening, headed north by a foot-hill trail, bypassing the Dempsey Ranch and finally reached the ice-covered Wisconsin Creek. As they crossed the ice broke ...they came out cold and wet and decided to stop and wait for daybreak. Without a fire, which could be seen, the only warmth they had was their horses and a few blankets. Daylight soon broke and they rode to the ranch where several men were still asleep.

They called for "Long John" Franck. He came out of a wickiup, half-asleep. Clark and Williams pushed him away from earshot of the others in the camp and questioned him. He declared no part in any killing, but they spotted Black Bess, the favorite mule Tbalt had ridden. Franck, when asked where the other two mules were, said he did not know. At this point the posse, cold, wet and irritable, were ready to hang Franck.

Williams intervened, warning not to act without more deliberation. He showed a stern, exceptional command over the men. Questioned further, Franck said he was afraid to tell anyone about the body or the mule. Asked why, he said he feared the man who had killed Tbalt...the other man in his wickiup. His frightened attitude convinced Williams and others they were close to getting Tbalt's killer. They asked him who it was. Franck hesitated, then stammered, *"George...George Ives!"*

Williams went back with several men and called Ives out of the hut. After a short and angry discussion, they told him he would have to come back to Nevada City with them and answer questions. *"All right,"* said Ives sourly, *"I expect I'll have to go."* The men of the posse searched the huts for guns. They found a hoard of guns, navy and dragoon revolvers, shotguns and rifles. Among them was one pistol, recognized as belonging to Leroy Southmayd, taken in a stage hold-up in late November (See Chapter 10).

"Long John" Franck was also taken prisoner at the ranch. George Hilderman was not in the immediate area. He would be found working on a bridge near the ranch and arrested as the posse headed back to town.

RACE TO ESCAPE...*no winner*

On the ride back to Nevada City, the prisoners were allowed to ride unencumbered, and Ives, a superb horseman, was certain he could outride anyone in the posse. He casually challenged his captors to a race. Several thought it would break the monotony of the long ride. Cunningly, Ives was sure he could outdistance them. He planned to reach Daley's ranch nearby, where he knew a fresh horse would be saddled and ready. Ives apparently told someone at the camp to sneak ahead and prepare his horse. However, Ives tired pony gave out before he reached the ranch. He abandoned the horse and ran into a ravine where he was recaptured at gunpoint. The men of the posse were tired...Ives' foolish two hour escape attempt only irritated them more. One of the posse said, *"Let's raise a pole and hang him... at once!"* Williams intervened and again saved Ives for a trial. [2] [3]

LIKEABLE...*but not drunk*

George Ives, not a common roust-about, had a prominent New England background. His parent's Inn, "Ives Grove," in Wisconsin, prospered and had grown into a tavern, restaurant and dance hall. Ives learned ranching and riding, until at eighteen, the California Gold Rush lured him away. He followed the gold camps and took to the taste of whiskey which made him obnoxious...and daring. He was polite and likable when sober, but ventured into dangerous situations when drunk.

Ives came to Bannack early in 1862, where he met Plummer. He later established a ranch at the north end of Alder Gulch. It was a legitimate business. However, Ives' ranch harbored a most nefarious crew, always suspicious and ready to prey on travelers who carried gold or anything of value. [4] [5]

The posse with their prisoner, George Ives, under heavy guard rode into Nevada City just after sunset. News of Ives' capture preceded the posse and "Clubfoot George" Lane hurriedly rode to Bannack to tell Plummer of Ives' capture and urged him to come back to Nevada City. Clubfoot George worked as a shoemaker in the Alder Gulch shop of Dance & Stuart and acted as spy for Plummer. Johnny Gibbons, rancher and another Plummer supporter, asked for the legal assistance of John D. Ritchie and H.P.A. Smith for Ives.

FIRST TRIAL...in Montana

Wilbur Sanders, while in Virginia City would build support for the formation of a new Territory. While he walked in Virginia City Sanders was approached by James Thurmond, who invited him to help defend the charges against Ives, Franck and Hilderman. Without reservations, he declined. He intended to make his way back to Bannack to spend Christmas with his wife and two sons.

The next morning, before boarding the stage to Bannack, Sanders was told the Lott brothers urgently wanted to see him. Upon arriving at their shop in Nevada City, John and Mortimer Lott implored Sanders to take the job as prosecutor in the Ives trial. It had been decided the town nearest the crime scene, Nevada City, would have jurisdiction over the trial.

Sanders had qualms about prosecuting a well known member of Henry Plummer's gang without irrefutable evidence. Plummer could control who would be jurors in a trial and if Ives escaped conviction, Sanders could be his next victim. He had little to gain, except...he was desperately needed. Not being afraid to accept a challenge, he recognized the offer by the Lott brothers as a chance to gain valuable experience.

He knew experience would give birth to success. Failure, however, also gives experience...learning what to avoid. Sanders understood the fear of failure leaves man void of accomplishment. Sanders inexperience as a prosecutor especially for murder, would be behind him and his career could proceed. As he later wrote in his memoirs, he reluctantly agreed to take the job...but decided he would, *"...push with utmost vigor, and if the guilt of the accused was certain, that the retribution would be swift and absolutely remorseless."* [6]

It was still winter but the sun worked hard to thaw the frozen gumbo off the streets. Sheriffs Hereford from Nevada City and Davis from Junction had a job to control the growing crowd. From 1,000 to 1,500 shivering people jammed the streets and building rooftops in Nevada City to attend the outdoor trial for the murder of their well-liked townsman, Nicholas Tbalt. The small number of men Hereford and Davis could recruit would be helped by James Williams, who led the posse to capture the men accused with the killing. Williams gathered men for guards, armed with rifles and shotguns, to control the large and growing crowd. Throughout the trial Wilbur Sanders watched the reaction of the crowd to tell if he was proceeding in the right direction.

THREATS...from a sheriff

It was December 19, 1863, when Sanders first encountered the crowd gathered in the soggy streets of Nevada City. Dr. Don Byam, a Dentist by trade, served as Judge for the trial. Sanders stood upon a freight wagon which had been moved into the street. He tried to organize the rules of order for the trial. Ives' lawyers shouted to be heard above the rousting response of the gathered swarm of onlookers.

It was agreed, after much arguing and deliberation, a pair of twelve-member juries would be chosen, one from Junction, the other from Nevada City. Sanders decided to deal with Ives' trial separately...and first. He had "Long John" Franck as his main witness, backed by George Hilderman...he would deal with their trial later.

Soon the throng of onlookers debated if lawyers should be allowed to participate. With the addition of Alexander Davis, Ives would have four counsels.

Atop the wagon with Dr. Byam, Sanders introduced himself as the nephew of Sidney Edgerton, the Presidentially-appointed Chief Justice of the new Idaho Territory. Confidence in the crowd grew and the intent of disallowing counsel was dropped.

Buzz Caven, Sheriff of Virginia City, brought forth a motion that a twelve-man jury from his town should also be named as a third advisory jury. Caven was thought to have ties with Plummer and would choose a jury of men partial to Ives. Sanders was adamantly opposed...and bluntly told Caven there was no reason for a third jury. Caven argued and waved a page of names chosen for a proposed third jury in Sanders' face. He asked Sanders, *"... what do you have against these men?"* Sanders replied he did not know any of them personally, but aware of their reputation, did not care to know any. Caven stood face to face with Sanders, eyes glaring, and said, *"I will personally hold you responsible for that remark!"* An unmistakable threat...but, Sanders would not back down...he would lose the support of the crowd! He stepped forward and staunchly told Caven he agreed to meet him in mortal conflict... *"but after the trial!"* The crowd backed Sanders and voted against Sheriff Caven's motion for a third jury. Sanders, had surely, gained the confidence of the crowd! [7]

Chapter Notes

Note 1. Professor Thomas Dimsdale later wrote of George Ives; "The carriage of this renowned desperado was sprightly, and his coolness was imperturbable. Long practice in confronting danger had made him absolutely fearless." He continued, "...the quick spirit which made him not only the terror of the community, but the dread of the band of ruffians with whom he was associated."

Office of Dr. Don L. Byam.
Dr. Byam served as judge in the murder trial of George Ives.

CHAPTER 13
GEORGE IVES' TRIAL
QUICKLY HANGED on HIS HISTORY
Mid-December, 1863

COURTROOM...open air

Judge Byam completed preliminaries for the trial's Saturday morning session and called a break for lunch. During the break a group of men prepared the semblance of an outdoor courtroom on the main street of Nevada City. The crowd watched from the sod-topped roofs of the adjoining cabins and buildings, or anywhere in the soggy streets they could find a dry spot. A large Schuttler wagon provided a somewhat proper podium for Judge Byam and Judge Wilson, both from the town of Junction. A second wagon was set up for the witnesses. A table and chair were placed nearby for the court recorder, William Pemberton, a lawyer from Virginia City. Benches for the jurors were gathered from the local saloons and hurdy-gurdy houses and set in a curve around the wagons. A bonfire to break the cold winter air was ablaze, yet Pemberton still needed gloves while he recorded the notes. [1]

SANDERS...meets Bagg

Sanders, unnerved by the "threat" from Sheriff Caven, took offensive remarks calmly, but had the feeling to respond in the same manner. In most part he lacked the cunning and ability necessary to avoid such retaliations. He could see and hear irritation rising in the crowd, possibly spawned by Ives' friends. Sanders anticipated fights, possibly with guns. In preparation, he borrowed a pair of Colt revolvers and put them in his coat pocket, one on each side.

Judge Wilson suggested Charles S. Bagg, a miner with a law degree, as someone who could help Sanders. Sanders knew the strength of Ives' team of lawyers and readily agreed to the offer. He knew Bagg would relate well with the crowd.

Sanders never forgot his first impression of Bagg and later wrote, *"...a short, stubbly, hairy, fatherly looking man, somewhat rude, of dilapidated garb, whose bootlegs did not have sufficient fiber to stand up, and into one of which he had vainly essayed to tuck one of the legs of his pantaloons."* He later insisted he was, *"...entirely satisfied"* with his partner who spoke intelligently and who reached the crowd so well. [2]

After lunch Ives was brought to the improvised court...with logging chains around his legs, locked with padlocks. He remained serene... ever-confident. He had friends in the crowd including "Tex" Crowell and Aleck Carter who shouted encouragement. Many in the crowd could not believe George Ives, a well mannered man, tall and handsome, could have killed young Tbalt. One of the nonbelievers was the court recorder, William Pemberton, who went on to serve as chief justice of Montana's territorial Supreme Court. He quite often had meetings and spoke with Ives in Virginia City. It is noted that Pemberton had written Ives did not drink...an error! Seeing Ives drunk would surely have changed his mind.
3

PROSECUTION...begins

Cocounsel Charles Bagg made the opening statement in the trial. Speaking to the jury members, he said they now had the opportunity to quell the robberies and killing that kept many from retaining their hard earned wealth. His first witness was William Palmer who had discovered Tbalt's frozen body. Palmer expressed the surprise and horror of the situation in a clear and understandable voice and told of his suspicion of Franck and Hildermann when they refused to help him load Tbalt's body into his wagon. His testimony brought forth the seriousness of the case and the impact it would have, not only against these three men, but for the townspeople. They would now be free from the fear they had known of Ives. This impact brought forth several men who testified they had been threatened or robbed by Ives. They told Sanders and Bagg of crimes not yet reported...because of fear. Their testimony brought forth a gruesome history of George Ives, heretofore unknown to the townspeople and hard for many to believe.

SHOOTINGS...before untold

Witnesses told of a killing by George Ives, on the trail to the Cold Springs ranch, in full view of ranch-hands at Daley's ranch. Ives met a man he considered to be a threat, and killed him in a deliberate, cold-blooded manner, shooting him in the head. When he fell from his horse, Ives led his horse away and left the body on the trail. Ranch-hands, who watched the shooting, buried the body in an unmarked grave.

Another witness told of a wanton attempt by Ives to kill during a robbery in 1862. Anton Holter, a Norwegian newcomer to Alder Gulch, had been stopped by two riders at gunpoint. With only a small amount of greenbacks, the robbers told Holter if he didn't have more money next time, they would shoot him! He was told he could leave, but as he mounted his horse, he heard the click of a revolver close to his head...and instinctively ducked. The shot tore through his hat, creased his scalp and knocked him off his horse. The shooter aimed for a second shot...but the gun misfired. Holter stumbled off the ground, ran and luckily escaped. He later described the shooter as George Ives! [4] [5] [6]

TROUBLE...no witness

Sanders and Bagg knew they had a problem...a weak case against Ives for the murder of Nick Tbalt. Long John Franck's testimony could be countered by defense counsel as self-serving ...to get himself free of any prosecution. Hildermann, another witness, was an old man and his weak testimony would easily be attacked by defense. The many newly reported claims from stage drivers, miners and others who had been accosted by Ives did nothing for Sander's murder trial of Tbalt, but they enforced the malevolent description of Ives' history.

Sanders needed hard, irrefutable evidence. There were no eyewitnesses to Tbalt's killing and Franck, as Sanders' only witness, could be lying. Sanders had no choice about Ives...hang him on his history...his past, murderous history. Would the crowd agree? Would the two juries agree?

WITNESSES...a gangly lot

Trial resumed Sunday morning, December 20, 1863. Sanders had to deal with a most obnoxious-looking Franck; he was tall, gangly and disheveled. One observer noted, *"He was one of the worst-looking men I have ever seen."*

Franck, as a witness, said that Tbalt came to retrieve two mules he had pastured at the nearby ranch. Ives, Tex Crowell and Carter watched Tbalt, as he paid for the pasturing from a pouch of gold he carried. When Tbalt left with the mules, Franck said he heard Ives remark to the group, *"...it was a shame to see him leave with such money and fine animals."* Franck continued his testimony and said they decided to toss a coin to see who would follow Tbalt and relieve him of his gold...Ives won. Ives mounted his horse, checked his guns and rode off, and returned only a short time later.

Franck stated to the court, Ives didn't want to shoot Tbalt in the back...he waited, and when Tbalt knelt to pray...Ives shot him in the head! Franck's brief testimony brought a torrent of claims from defense counsel...Franck served his own purpose in "peaching" on Ives. Although

Franck adamantly claimed he was not part of the crime, the crowd wanted him hung... no matter how innocent he might be! [7]

The cache of weapons recovered from the hut included a revolver belonging to Leroy Southmayd, sold to him by Amos Hall. Ives' possession of the gun proved he was involved with the Southmayd robbery, but bore no evidence in Tbalt's murder trial, other than to add to Ives evil background. His "persona non grata" aspect grew and spread among the crowd. The talk amongst the people about Ives, and his cohorts, had reached the level where some of Ives' friends made themselves less apparent. Aleck Carter and "Tex" Crowell, earlier in the crowd, were also nowhere to be seen. Did they desert Ives? Or were they preparing to regroup? Where was Plummer? A Nevada City bartender claimed he had served Plummer during the trial, but no one else in the bar saw him. [8]

HANG HIM ON HIS HISTORY...a plan

Sanders planned to execute George Ives by hanging for Tbalt's killing and his nefarious history of criminal plunder in the area, but defense counsel strongly objected. Accounts of numerous robberies that had nothing to do with the Tbalt murder and "hearsay" evidence, all made their way into the court...and heard by the crowd! The defense tried to counter his hanging by bringing witnesses to provide an alibi for Ives. Witness accounts for Ives' whereabouts at the time of the shooting failed...mainly because no one knew when Tbalt had been killed. Ives decided not to testify in his own behalf...which was curious. Why should this smooth-tongued, well appearing gentleman, not trust his own ability to swoon some portion of the jury...because he knew of his guilt? Sanders, well aware of Ives' guilt, had prepared his case well!

There was slim evidence in the murder case of Nicholas Tbalt. Sanders, however, laid before the twenty-four members of advisory jurists, a number of other facts against Ives in his criminal past.

Sanders later wrote, *"I cannot think that the testimony introduced to that assemblage left a particle of doubt in the mind of any spectator of the following five facts:*

1st. That Ives killed Tbalt as charged.

2nd. That he had committed a half dozen other murders in the vicinity of equal cruelty.

3rd. That he was the leading actor in robbing the stage passengers between Rattlesnake Ranch and Bannack in October, when Dan McFadden, Leroy Southmayd and others were passengers.

102

4th. That he had pursued the vocation of a highway robber for a number of months along the roads to Salt Lake City.

5th. That he belonged to the criminal classes, and that his appetite for blood had grown til it became a consuming passion." [9]

Judge Byam adjourned court for the day, to reopen in the morning with closing statements from counsel.

102 KILLINGS.....people were afraid

Nicholas Tbalt had gone on the trail alone that fatal day carrying a pouch of gold. He showed the gold, unsuspectingly, to a rough crowd when he paid his grazing bill at Long John's ranch. Then he disappeared...missing for nine days. If his body had not been found he would have become another of the many "missing" reported by Dimsdale of the *Montana Post.*

Professor Thomas Dimsdale had reported one-hundred-two missing or murdered men in his 1867 book, *The Vigilantes of Montana.* This figure sounds high, but Dimsdale had a propensity for elaborating newsworthy items to the fullest. It was of public interest to read of the holdups and possible killing of miners who made their riches in the gold fields of Bannack and Alder Gulch. Many were never heard from again, even by relatives back home. Without any word about leaving, many gold-seekers just dropped out of sight. "Bummer" Dan McFadden might well have been one of those unlucky souls. He could have encountered Ives while walking on the trail to catch the stage, been robbed, shot and his body dumped in a ravine never to be found. (See Chapter 10).

These killings were of concern and brought fear to many of the citizens. There were those, like Anton Holter, who had escaped the wrath of Plummer and Ives, but were fearful to say anything. If a robbery victim reported anything to Plummer, the Sheriff, it would have been a death knell for the victim.

FOUNDATION LAID...against killers

The Dimsdale calculations of killings cannot be corroborated. He had no list of names or accounting, but the number of murders has crept down through the annals of history...although many writers and historians have disputed it. For the short time Plummer, Ives, and their cohorts, had been in the Bannack and the Alder Gulch gold region, it does seem high. As today, the press seems to have expounded the fear of the people. Dimsdale later notes, *"It was the finger of God that indicated the scene of the assassination, and it was His will stirring in the hearts of honest and indignant gazers on the ghastly remains of Tbalt that organized the party which, though not then formally enrolled as a Vigilance Committee, was the nucleus and embryo of the order..."* [10]

Fear of reprisal was heavy among the townspeople. The trial of Ives for the brutal killing of Tbalt was the beginning of the end to their fear and the people sensed it. That "order" would bring historic fame for some, infamy for others.

While he worked on closing statements, Sanders was called to a meeting in Virginia City by Nicholas Wall. In the back room of Nye & Kenna's dry goods store, Sanders and Wall met with John Nye, Alvin Brookie and Paris Pfouts. Sanders met with these men previously and had discussed a subject of profound importance, something they planned would take place...after the trial.

CLOSING...to a dead end

Sanders did not sleep well Sunday night. The next morning, December 21, 1863, the crowd began to collect around the outdoor courtroom, on rooftops of adjoining cabins, anywhere they could hear well. Sanders could sense the impatience of the crowd...they wanted summation... and a hanging! Sanders described Ives' killing of Tbalt as "devious and merciless." He pointed out other killings and robberies Ives had committed. He was the leader in the robberies of Leroy Southmayd and Bummer Dan. Sanders depicted Ives as a common thief in the past...now he turned to spilling blood.

The defense counsel did their best to rebut Sanders accusations, as well as to attack him personally. Time had passed for the closing statements and the crowd became impatient. Finally Judges Byam and Wilson instructed the two juries, twelve men each, to adjourn and begin deliberation. They would give an "advisory" verdict, but the jury of the whole, the crowd, would have the final word!

After short deliberation the two juries returned. All but one juror, Henry Spivey, voted "guilty!" Sanders knew in the past only one juror could cause a mistrial. He made a quick motion to the jury of the whole to, *"...adopt and approve the verdict of guilty."* Before the defense could object, Judge Byam accepted the motion and turned to the crowd of excited onlookers, who loudly voiced their opinion...they agreed!

Again, before defense counsel could muster the jury, Sanders called for them to pass sentence on Ives, *"...that he be hanged by the neck until dead."* Byam again called for a vote and again the crowd shouted approval. The defense was stunned...and George Ives faced the hangman's noose! Sheriffs Hereford and Davis were ordered to find a suitable site to carry out Ives' execution. [11]

DELAY OF DEATH...denied

George Ives solemnly stood up, climbed onto the wagon and clenched Sanders forearm. Guards quickly stepped forward, aimed their shotguns at Ives...and the crowd fell silent. *"Colonel Sanders,"* Ives began, *"I'm a gentleman and I believe you are one and I want to ask a favor which you alone can grant. If our places were changed I know I would grant it to you. I've been pretty wild, I admit, but my people know nothing of it. I have a mother and a couple of sisters in Wisconsin and I want time to write them a letter and to make my will. If you will have this execution postponed until tomorrow morning I give you my word of honor as a gentleman that I will not try to escape and that I will not permit my friends to interfere in this matter in any way."*

Sanders stood silent, looked into Ives' blue eyes and pondered what to say. He had never committed anyone to death before. Ives request brought unforseen events that could bear heavily on his mind. He didn't know exactly what to say. From an adjoining rooftop came the stern voice of John "X" Biedler. *"Sanders,"* he shouted, *"Ask him how long he gave the Dutchman!"*

"Ives," Sanders somberly replied, *"You should have thought of this before. You still have a few minutes. Get down and start your letter and I'll put a motion about your property that I think will be satisfactory to you."* Ives' request to live another day was denied. He returned to his seat and was given paper and pencil by one of his counsel.

A pole was braced against the base of an unfinished log building, just steps away from the "courtroom," and the hangman's noose secured. Ives, after writing a few words to his family, was led to the makeshift gallows, lifted onto a dry goods crate and the noose placed around his neck. Judge Byam asked if he had any final words. Ives replied with concern, *"I am innocent of this crime."* and added, *"Aleck Carter killed the Dutchman."* Sanders called out, *"Men, do your duty,"* and the crate was kicked from under Ives feet. Judge Byam waited a moment, the crowd hushed, then he walked to Ives limp body, reached up and said, *"His neck is broken....He is dead."* [12] [13]

Sanders called out, "Men do your duty."

There now remains a question in history...was it Ives...or Carter...that killed Tbalt? Long John Franck, at the ranch that cold winter morning, pointed the evil finger of guilt at Ives...not Carter. Put in such a life-threatening situation, if not telling the truth, would he accuse the man he feared the most...Ives, or the least...Carter? Why did George Ives claim Carter as the killer? Is it that Ives saw Aleck Carter abandon him during the trial and was trying to "get even?"

To close out the trial Hildermann, defended by H.P.A. Smith, was banished from the area with one provision; after ten days anyone seeing him east of the Bitterroot Mountains could shoot him! Plummer later asked Hildermann to stay in Bannack and work for him, but the offer was denied. For Long John Franck's testimony against Ives, he was set free, but required to ride with the first Vigilante posse to capture Aleck Carter.

"Tex" Crowell and Carter had attended the trial, but when Ives' fate became apparent, they left the area. Crowell had been questioned earlier by Sanders and determined no charges against him would be enforced. With Ives' final words Aleck Carter would become the person of interest in the coming days.

SANDERS WINS...round one

Less than an hour after being convicted of the murder of Nicholas Tbalt, George Ives was hung! It was the beginning of the threshold for a new "peoples" law for what would soon become the new Montana Territory. A posse would be formed by a new *"Vigilance Committee"* to pursue the remainder of Plummer's gang of "Innocents."

For the next forty-two days, through one of the coldest winters in the area, it would be the hardest test of the will of twenty-four new volunteer members of the "Vigilantes." They were to catch and deal, what has been called a "ruthless" blow, to rid the evil forced upon them over the past two years.

Wilbur Sanders would have to rely upon the criminal history of George Ives to convict him. Now he and the Vigilance Committee would use that theory of justice to convict other road agents and killers aligned with Plummer. "Hard evidence" was difficult to find in the lawless community. They would have to rely upon "hearsay evidence" from people they knew and trusted to corral and convict the remainder of Plummer's gang.

Colonel Sanders with three volunteers from Bannack, five from Virginia City, and several from Nevada City, would establish a secretive group that became known to be a nemesis to criminals...for years to come.

REVENGE...prosecutor's life at risk

During a lapse in the trial, Sanders sat in John Creighton's store quietly reading when a known "rough," Harvey Meade, came in and confronted him. Meade, a desperado who once planned the seizure of a Federal gold shipment in San Francisco, had a revolver tucked in his belt. He faced Sanders and started swearing and calling him names in a loud, boisterous voice. A customer, also casually reading, expected an imminent clash between the two. He reached into a tool barrel and pulled out a heavy pick handle. Sanders cautiously reached into his coat pocket and cocked his derringer.

Looking up at Meade, Sanders quietly stated, *"Harvey, I should feel hurt if some men said this; but from such a dog as you it is not worth noticing!"* John Creighton walked up behind Meade and said, *"You have to get out of here...quick!"* Meade saw his dangerous disadvantage, turned and left the store...disturbed and foiled. Sanders slipped his gun back into his pocket and returned to reading. [14]

REVENGE FOILED...an accident occurs

After Ives execution, William Pemberton, who recorded notes for the trial, recalled he heard three of Ives' cohorts talking, *"Let's take him back of the house and kill him."* Not knowing who they were talking about, Pemberton paid little attention. When Sanders walked up, one of the men said, *"Yonder he stands, now."* Another said, *"I will call him."* In answer to the call, Sanders passed by Pemberton, who warned him not to go near them. Sanders, nonchalant about the matter, calmly said, *"I guess they won't kill me."* Disturbed, Pemberton asked Sanders if he was armed. Sanders said he was and unnerved, walked toward the men. Pemberton cautiously followed. One man said, *"We want to see you back here..."* and pointed between two adjoining log houses. They walked into a passageway at the rear of the cabins. Pemberton cautiously followed a few steps behind...suddenly he heard a gunshot! All three men hurriedly scattered. Pemberton ran forward expecting to see Sanders on the ground, dead! Instead, he saw Sanders beating the pocket of his coat...it was on fire!

Expecting to be killed, Sanders had attempted to pull his pistol, but it accidently discharged while still in his pocket. The shot scared the would-be killers into fleeing...and saved Sanders' life, possibly Pemberton's as well. [15]

Sanders accident did not distract him. His determined veracity remained for his formation of a committee...a union of dedicated leaders banded together to crush relentless members of Henry Plummer's gang. It seemed the only way to stop their devastation upon the citizenry of Alder Gulch and Bannack. An end to the killing, robbing and rowdiness... was about to begin!

Chapter Notes

Note 1. Anton Holter, after his brief skirmish with Ives, became a leading businessman and a Bank Director in Helena, Montana.

CHAPTER 14
VIGILANCE COMMITTEE
MONTANA ROOTS
December, 1863-64

Wilbur F. Sanders tried his first case in an area with no dedicated law or enforcement. He put his expertise to work and succeeded in convicting George Ives for the murder of Nicholas Tbalt. The killing gave the townspeople a determined courage to stand up to Plummer's gang.

Sanders met with Paris Pfouts and several anxious shopkeepers at Nye & Kenna's store in Virginia City. They met to determine a way to combat the errant criminal activity such as the senseless killing of young Tbalt. They had to stop the slurry of crime and the fear that plagued the people of the area. First they had to formulate and define guidelines, or the by-laws, for their volunteer group of miners, shopkeepers and ranchers.

MONTANA VIGILANTES...the birth

A meeting was called with John Lott at his store in Nevada City and the creation of a special committee began. The framework of area citizens would unite to form a new combat team with a determined, even ruthless, intent to crush the growing criminal faction.

On December 23, 1863, two days after the George Ives' hanging, John Lott and William "Old Man" Clark felt Aleck Carter played a major role in the killing of young Nicholas Tbalt...he must be captured...and justice due must be paid!

At the meeting a hurriedly written document was prepared... pledging honor among members that no laws should be violated. Most importantly, all volunteer members were sworn to a code of secrecy. It was signed by twenty-four men, including Lott, Clark and James "Cap" Williams.

Paris Pfouts was chosen as President of the Vigilance Committee. James Williams was voted Executive Officer and John Lott as Secretary/ Treasurer. Wilbur Sanders was chosen as Prosecuting Officer. A full set of contemporary by-laws and regulations, describing the Vigilance Committee's mission and duties was formulated. The Committee would have the final word. There would be no appeals and, *"The only punishment that shall be inflicted by this Committee is DEATH."*

A "Company" of members was formed for each of the mining camps, with leaders or "Captains" chosen by the men of each company. The membership of the Vigilantes grew to the point where the "roughs" were now afraid to brag to anyone as they had before. The threat of fear had flip-flopped to the Vigilantes' favor!

FIRST JOB...catch Carter

James "Cap" Williams led the Vigilante Posse to capture Aleck Carter, but this time they prepared for the harsh December weather. They wore layers of clothing, heavy coats and carried bedrolls with warm blankets. Most carried pistols, some two, plus a rifle or shotgun. The large volunteer posse proceeded north past McCartney Mountain, flanking the Pioneer Range, then headed north to Cottonwood camp in the Deer Lodge Valley. On the way they met a rider headed south..."Red" Yeager. Asked if he knew the whereabouts of Aleck Carter, Yeager nodded and replied, *"... there were a bunch with Carter, all drunk."* When the posse arrived at Cottonwood they found Carter and his group had already fled. Williams thought this was strange...why would they leave camp and go into the freezing cold, wintery hills...especially in a drunken state...were they warned? Possibly Yeager had alerted them and lied about it. The posse stayed a couple of days at Cottonwood to rest weary horses and mules. They decided not to pursue Carter into the frozen, snow-covered mountains.

On December 28, the posse headed back south. The weather was cold, far below freezing. Eventually they crossed the Big Hole River and reached Beaverhead Rock on the Beaverhead River when the weather turned mean and cold...Montana cold...with blizzard conditions and deep, drifting snow. Williams decided to camp and wait out the storm. The camp site afforded no adequate firewood and the horses were set loose to forage on their own. While waiting for the storm to let up, Williams huddled in his bedroll and pondered what Yeager had told him. Did he lie? Was he a member of Plummer's gang?

When the storm subsided the posse retrieved the animals that survived and rode to the well-traveled trail between Bannack and Alder Gulch. On the trail the group met "X" Beidler, who had been searching for an overdue wagon train from Salt Lake City. Beidler told Williams of having met with Buck Stinson and Ned Ray while in Bannack, and that they had talked about Red Yeager at the Rattlesnake Ranch. This convinced Williams to split from the posse and go back to the Ranch where Yeager had been known to work.

At the ranch, Williams pounded on the door and came face to face with Buck Stinson…gun in hand. Stinson backed off when Williams told him he was looking for Yeager…not him. Stinson told Williams that Yeager was in a wickiup behind the ranch-house. Both Stinson and Ned Ray then hurriedly left the ranch and rode towards Bannack. Williams found Yeager asleep in the wickiup. When Williams told him he was under arrest, Yeager surrendered quietly. Williams decided not to brave the cold and stay the night at the deserted ranch with his prisoner.

In the morning Williams took Yeager and rode to the Dempsey ranch on the Stinking Water River where he rejoined the rest of the posse. Williams soon learned George Brown was also at the ranch and remembered he had given false testimony at the trial in an attempted alibi for Ives. Williams told his men to watch Brown, while he talked with Yeager. Under serious questioning by Williams, Yeager broke down and admitted he had carried a note warning Carter to, *"Get up and dust, and lie low for black ducks,"* but he claimed Brown had written the note.

After all their riding, suffering the cold and blizzards to capture Carter, the posse was furious to learn Yeager and Brown had warned him. Williams took the men of the posse to a nearby bridge and called for a vote. The posse voted both should be hung!

Williams doubted the couple had committed a crime serious enough for a hanging. Rather than hang the pair, he ordered they be taken to Virginia City to face Paris Pfouts and a tribunal. This did not sit well with the posse, but Williams, with strong hand and a cool head, prevailed…for now. Yeager and Brown were taken by several of the posse to Laurin's Ranch, just a few miles north of Virginia City. Close to nightfall Williams caught up with his men and their prisoners. Tired, both physically and mentally, he decided to catch some well deserved rest. Meanwhile, the posse renewed their desire to hang both Yeager and Brown. They woke up Williams and sleepy-eyed, he reluctantly agreed to the posse's demand.

"RED'S" TALE…good as gold

Williams woke Yeager and Brown, but before he could tell them the bad news, Yeager calmly said, "I know I'm going to die…I'm going to be hanged." Williams, still not in full agreement the two should hang, silently nodded his head in affirmation.

Yeager continued, *"It is pretty rough, but I deserved this years ago. What I wanted to say is that I know all about this gang, and there are men in it that deserve this more than I do. But I should die happy if I could see them hanged, or know that it would be done. I don't say this to get off. I don't want to get off."*

Men in the posse, eager to get proof against Plummer, told Yeager he had the power to stop the crime and killing...if he told all he knew about Plummer and his gang.

"Red" Yeager hesitated, but provided the names of the conspirators, from Henry Plummer as chief to "Clubfoot George" Lane, as well as the gang's secret operations. Williams told one of the posse to write down all the names and information Yeager would give.

What Yeager knew...he told. If what he told were not lies, his information would be invaluable to Williams and the Vigilance Committee. However, Williams made a mistake. After hearing Yeager tell what he knew...he hanged both of them!

After watching Brown being hanged, "Red" Yeager's last words were, *"Good-bye boys; God bless you. You are on a good undertaking."*
1 2

Chapter Notes

Note 1. The Vigilante document, signed by members at John Lott's store in Nevada City, has survived, more than 145 years, and remains today in the archives of the Montana Historical Society in Helena, Montana. In the Vigilance Committee's declaration of punishment, the emphasis of capital letters ("DEATH") is part of the original quotation.

Note 2. Erastus "Red" Yeager had grown up on a farm in Iowa and was known for his bright red hair. He came west with the surge of gold strikes in the Rocky Mountains and knowing animals, became a freighter. He joined "Doc" Howard's group on the way to Bannack and met Frank Thompson on the trip. He had known James and Granville Stuart during his younger years in Iowa.

Note 3. The following excerpts by Davis and Pfouts were given later regarding the formation of the "combat" group above:

Adriel B. Davis was one of the original twelve who signed the by-laws. He gave the following account; "The meeting was called by Paris Pfouts and Sanders; when we got there it was suggested that we organize a Vigilante Committee for self protection. Among those present were Wilbur Sanders, Paris Pfouts, James Williams, J. M. Fox, A. B. Davis, John S. Lott, Elkanah Morse, and a young man who clerked in McClurg's store, whose name I have forgotten and can't get, but he was from California and was the one who administered the oath to us."

Paris Pfouts wrote the following account of the meeting in his memoirs long after leaving Montana: "An oath of secrecy was administered to all and a plan of organization discussed. I and Colonel Sanders were for immediate and decisive action, but no conclusion was definitely arrived at. We continued our meetings and in the course of three or four days the number was increased to about 50, and all among the best and most reliable citizens of Virginia City, and in the mining camps surrounding it, when they resolved upon selection of a president or 'chief.'" 3

Note 4. Questions arise among historians and writers concerning "Red" Yeager's confession. The document Williams directed one of his men to write, containing names of gang members exposed by Yeager, has yet to be found. Key documents of the Vigilance Committee were staunchly preserved…but Yeager's list is missing.

Yeager may have confessed to what he knew, but it may have been limited and later revised or expounded by someone, possibly Thomas Dimsdale, who was an advocate and defender of the Vigilante movement, but not an acknowledged member. He may have used Yeager's confession to add and expose names and incidents of which he had knowledge about the conspirators…but had fear of gang repercussion. Working with the Vigilance committee, Dimsdale could have revealed his information as coming from the dead Yeager…the source could hardly be disputed. There were reported to be four copies of "Red" Yeagers list, but apparently none have survived.

In many writings about the Vigilantes, especially by Dimsdale, the names of individual members were not disclosed. Some members did not want notoriety for fear of retaliation by Plummer's gang members. Dimsdale would use numbers rather than names. At the time, secrecy was of importance, but it also discreetly hid some of the heroism and determination of many of the well deserving members of the Vigilance Committee.

Gravestone bearing Masonic symbol.

CHAPTER 15
HANG 'EM...on THEIR HISTORY
BANNACK...A COLD DAY
Midwinter, 1863-64

WANTED...crooks of all kinds

James Williams and the posse were dog-tired upon their arrival back at Nevada City. They did not succeed in their plan to capture Aleck Carter...but may have acquired much more in their capture and confession of Yeager.

Williams and John Lott proceeded to Virginia City and sought out Paris Pfouts, the President of the newly formed Vigilance Committee. They shared information of their trip over the past two weeks with Pfouts and Colonel Sanders. They hoped Yeager's list naming Sheriff Henry Plummer and names of his gang members could be used. This would render some valuable information and validate their new organization's need and use of secrecy among questionable new volunteer members.

They could now formulate a list of wanted gang members such as this:

WANTED FOR MURDER OR ROBBERY
Dutch John Wagner & Steve Marshland....Moody Wagon Train Robbery
Bill Bunton & Frank Parish...Robbery of "Bummer Dan" McFadden
Bob Zachary, Bill Graves & George Ives...Leroy Southmayd Robbery
"Doc" Howard, Chris Lowry, Jim Romaine & Billy Page....Murder of Lloyd Magruder and four of his men
Henry Plummer, Buck Stinson & Ned Ray...Accomplices...All of the above

PLUMMER...feels the heat

The suspicion of Plummer had grown among Committee members in Alder Gulch, but not in Bannack. News about the conviction of Ives and the Yeager confession, made it seventy miles to Bannack, as though the telegraph was already in full operation in the area.

Plummer was very nervous knowing the Vigilance Committee would be coming for him. He started spreading a rumor the Vigilantes were coming not only for him...but also for some of the outstanding citizens in Bannack...such as his friend and landlord, George Crisman. Plummer needed worthy people on his side. He hoped to put a coerced fear, of the Vigilantes, in the minds of the citizens...it might do the trick against his oncoming "swarm of killers."

Frank Thompson, a boarder with Plummer, still had reservations about this affable man's ability to commit crime. However, there were times when he questioned Plummer's whereabouts, and it troubled him. He recalled Plummer's being "missing" at times major robberies took place.

The last straw, for Thompson's doubt, came one afternoon when Plummer entered his store. Shortly after, a driver of the Oliver & Company stage-line also stopped by. *"Immediately"* Thompson recounted, *"Both men began to fumble for their guns...I saw there was going to be trouble."* After the Southmayd robbery on the stage-line, all the drivers were tense in the presence of Plummer. Cursing loudly, the two men started at each other. Three women were in the store shopping, but as the altercation heated up, they ran out.

Thompson abruptly stepped between the two men and pushed Plummer to the rear of the store. Angered, Plummer pulled his Bowie knife from the scabbard under his coat and took a swing at Thompson...but just missed! Thompson furiously pushed Plummer out the back door of the store and slammed it shut. The disdained driver left out the front of the store with increased hate of Plummer. Thompson witnessed Plummer's vicious temper and began to rethink his cast of the "pleasant and agreeable" sheriff.

Later in Nevada City, north of Alder Gulch, Colonel Sanders started the murder trial of Plummer's friend and gang member, George Ives. Thompson anticipated a conviction of Ives and reflected on the trial, *"This may have been the reason Plummer was on edge..."* and questioned, *"...but why did he attack me!?"* Plummer had good reason to be edgy and deeply concerned...an Ives' conviction would implicate him! [1]

After Paris Pfouts and the Vigilance Committee reviewed Yeager's list of gang members, with Plummer's name at the top, it was decided by the Committee, the best place to seek retribution for Plummer's crimes would be Bannack....to arrest and execute the members of his gang.

TO BANNACK...recruit members

In early January, John Lott and three members of the Vigilance Committee went to Bannack to recruit local members. Even with Yeager's damning list of gang members' names, it would be difficult to convince some Bannack residents about Plummer. Most had voted Plummer to Sheriff and knew this amiable man personally. Lott would have a hard job to convince the citizens of Bannack that Plummer, with his deputies, deserved to be punished.

116

Plummer anticipated a posse coming after him and sent several of his gang to ambush them. Plummer's men waited under a bridge along the trail, but the extreme cold cut their plan short...they gave up their ambush and headed back to town to get warm. Only minutes later Lott and his small group rode across the bridge and into Bannack.

Meanwhile, Neil Howie came to Bannack with his partner John Fetherstun and their prisoner from the Moody wagon train robbery, "Dutch John" Wagner. Plummer met with Howie earlier and demanded Wagner be turned over to him, but Howie refused, aware of the Vigilante presence in Bannack. Several of John Lott's Vigilante recruits met with Fetherstun in Durant's saloon and took charge of Wagner. Both Howie and Fetherstun were relieved and joined forces with the Bannack Vigilantes. Lott and his men interrogated Wagner and determined he should be hanged for his part in the Moody wagon train robbery. Had Wagner implicated Plummer, and corroborated Yeager's list of gang members, Lott would have no problem convincing the Bannack citizens of Plummer's guilt.

SCARE TACTIC...poor idea

Colonel Wilbur Sanders, concerned about the lack of belief some Bannack members had in Plummer's guilt, devised a shrewd plan; convince Plummer the Vigilantes would, without any doubt, hang him! When Plummer would get his horse and start to flee...shoot him! Sanders had discussed this plan with Sidney Edgerton. But after deliberation... as written later by Edgerton's daughter, Mattie, who had overheard their discussion, "...this seemed to appear more unlawful than previous hangings...the idea was abandoned."

Several new members were recruited and sworn into the newly formed Vigilantes of Bannack. Henry Tilden retold them about his past "robbery" in Horse Prairie by Plummer. New members secretly agreed to the guilt and punishment of Sheriff Henry Plummer and deputies Buck Stinson and Ned Ray. By noon, Sanders and Lott had recruited several new Vigilante members. However, George Crisman, the merchant who rented office space to Plummer, plus other notable townsmen, still opposed charges made against Plummer.

Some history writers have attempted to depict Plummer as "not guilty" because of the Vigilante's use of "hearsay," instead of hard evidence. One-hundred forty years ago, word of a respected person in the community was accepted as "hard evidence."

117

A "miner's court" was also deemed as good as trial by jury...even by some of the accused. The Vigilance Committee would not interfere with a working system of justice...only when that system failed.

COLD...damned cold

On Sunday morning, January 10, 1864, the weather turned bitter cold. Thermometers registered forty-two degrees below zero, some even broke. Frank Thompson ate breakfast at the Vail household as usual, with his partner Joseph Swift, Martha Jane Vail and her two children,...and Henry Plummer. Thompson was the only one at the table who knew of the "secret" plans that day for the suspicious Plummer. Thompson had trouble eating breakfast, fighting off temptations to warn him. Plummer, also not feeling well, stayed at the Vail home most of the day trying to rest...and think.

After working until late in the day at his store, Thompson walked home. He stopped at Edgerton's cabin and knowing Vigilante plans he cancelled his regular Sunday choir practice.

About dusk the stomping of boots across the Grasshopper Creek footbridge was loud and ominous. A large posse of Vigilantes split into two groups. One group led by William Roe, headed south to Toland's cabin in Yankee Flats, where Buck Stinson was known to stay. They surrounded the cabin and with little trouble, arrested Stinson. He hollered and swore vile, obscene remarks at the posse, to no avail. Frank Sears and Harry King captured Ned Ray, passed out drunk on a gambling table in a Yankee Flats saloon. He tried to fight, but found it useless.

The second posse surrounded Vail's cabin, just north of Grasshopper Creek. John Lott led the group and knocked on the door. Martha Vail answered and was politely pushed aside. Lott moved inside where he saw Plummer on the bed. It was unusual to see Plummer resting...and unarmed! He had taken off his pistol and knife and laid them under his coat on a nearby chair. Lott saw the pistol and quickly stepped between Plummer and the chair and grabbed the gun. He handed Plummer his coat and ordered him outside where Vigilante guards waited.

Plummer feared what was about to happen. He cleared his throat as if to speak, but Lott angrily pushed him to the door. As Plummer pulled on his coat, he looked at Vail's wife, she was bewildered! He gave her the lame excuse he had to attend to the newly captured Wagner. Outside, two men grabbed Plummer's arms and quickly pulled him away from the cabin.

118

Nearby, guards tied the hands of Stinson and Ray. Stinson continued ranting and swearing. Plummer saw the panic in their eyes, realized the seriousness of the situation and knew, he too, faced dire consequences!

Colonel Sanders heard Plummer weakly call to him. Sanders walked up to Plummer and stared directly at Plummer, face to face, and in a stern unemotional voice told him, *"It is useless for you to beg for your life; that affair is settled and cannot be altered. You are to be hanged!...but I cannot help it...if I would."*

Plummer, never fully aware he faced death, now feared the ultimate and pleaded, *"Oh, men, for God's sake, don't hang me! Banish me! I'll leave the country forever and you'll never see me again! Do anything to me, only don't hang me!"*

Sanders, not desiring to speak to the sniveling Plummer, instead disgustedly called out to the Vigilante guards. *"...March!..."* ordering them to take the prisoners up the street toward Cemetery Hill...and the gallows!

Plummer stammered weakly, *"You men know us better than this!"*... but no one listened. Although that January night was far below freezing, none of the doomed men were concerned with the severe cold...nor did the Vigilante guards...they had a job to do!

Facing death earlier, when shot by Crawford, Plummer's voice was stern and demanding...but now his voice was feeble...stammering. His thoughts could have raced back to his earlier experiences with the Vigilantes in San Francisco. He learned then and realized now, the Vigilantes were not to be challenged...they were deadly determined! Plummer was, as well noted later by Sanders, *"...loathsome in his abject and abandoned cowardice."*

HANGMAN'S GULCH...three reservations

Plummer, with Stinson and Ray, were marched up the main street of Bannack, then north into the gulch below Cemetery Hill. Plummer had earlier erected the gallows to hang Peter Horan...but not himself.

Continually Plummer pled for mercy, *"Oh God, I'm too wicked to die!"* He sobbed, searching for something to stop the ultimate... *"Please don't hang me!"* His eyes woefully pierced the crowd gathered below the gallows, with the desperate hope to see someone, anyone...who could help him!

Three ropes, each with a hangman's noose, were thrown over the cross beam of the gallows. A small crowd shivered in the freezing wind blowing down the gulch...those on-lookers who felt the bitter cold left... the cold-hearted ones stayed!

Ned Ray was brought up first...still trying to break loose. The guards had to struggle to place the noose around his neck. Lifted by two men, just before being dropped, Ray wriggled his right hand free and stuck his fingers under the noose, only painfully prolonging the ultimate. Dropped, he kicked at the end of the rope, choking, until one of the hangmen grabbed his arm and sternly yanked his hand free from the noose. Ray's body jerked, then became still...dead still! Stinson on the ground beneath the gallows moaned, *"There goes poor Ned...!"*

The hangman motioned to the guards to bring up Stinson. As the guards lifted Buck Stinson up to the noose, he tried one last chance to avoid death. He desperately called out, *"I'll confess...!"* Plummer, as if he accepted the deadly situation, yelled at Stinson, *"We've done enough already... twice over... to send us to hell!"*

Stinson was also unlucky...as he was dropped by the guards, the noose slipped! Rather than breaking his neck for a quick, painless end, he spent his last few minutes kicking, squirming...finally choking to death.

Henry Plummer still pleaded nervously, shifting his stance to face each of his guards. He avoided looking at the two lifeless bodies hanging on the gallows above him. He saw a friend, George Crisman, in the crowd and moaned to him for help, *"Please!"* Crisman answered, *"No Henry, we can't do anything for you."*

The hangman's stern voice broke the silence, *"Bring up Plummer!"* A shudder racked through Plummer's frail body. Grabbed by the guards, Plummer fell to his knees in the snow. *"Give a man time to pray!"* he cried hopelessly. *"Certainly"* replied the hangman, *"But do your praying up there,"* as he nodded to the two cold, limp forms above him. Plummer stared up at the two lifeless bodies of Stinson and Ray...and suddenly became somber and quiet.

The hangman removed Plummer's scarf from his neck. Plummer grabbed it and threw it to Joseph Swift, at the edge of the crowd, saying, *"Take this... remember me...!"* The young man fell to the ground sobbing. Swift had been a staunch admirer of Plummer since their meeting at Sun River.

As the guard tied his hands and placed the noose over his head, Plummer solemnly turned to him and pleaded, *"Give me a good drop!"* After watching both Ray and Stinson kick and struggle to their death, Plummer feared the ultimate but knew a *"good drop"* would mean a quick, and hopefully, painless end.

On January 10, 1864, a miserably cold night, two men lifted Henry Plummer as high as they could...and dropped him...he died instantly! [2] [3] [4]

Frank Thompson, not wishing to witness his former acquaintance executed, stayed at the Edgerton residence. After the hanging, he was told... *"It is all over!"* Thompson went to Vail's cabin and told Martha Vail about Plummer. She fainted and fell to the floor.

Chapter Notes

Note 1. Sometime after Pfouts received Yeager's news about Plummer he wrote, "After acquiring a full knowledge of these facts, from confessions of members of the band and other sources, the Executive Committee decided that parties (of Vigilantes) should be sent from Virginia City to Bannack City."

Note 2. Dimsdale later wrote in his book, *Vigilantes of Montana*, about the hanging of Plummer, Stinson and Ray. "The 'Reign of terror' in Bannack was over!" Sheriff Plummer would be the first and only elected Official hanged in the Montana Territory. Ray, with Stinson, had attempted the robbery of Leroy Southmayd and was wanted in Salt Lake City. Stinson had been involved in the shooting of Sheriff Dillingham and had earlier killed "Old Snag," a Bannock Indian.

Note 3. In Idaho, the murder trial against the killers of Lloyd Magruder and friends was about to close. Billy Page had testified against others, hence he did not receive a penalty. The other three, David Renton (alias Doc Howard), Chris Lowry and James Romaine were convicted and hanged in Idaho on March 4, 1864. (See Chapter 9).

Dance & Stuart General Merchandise storefront, Virginia City.

CHAPTER 16
VIRGINIA CITY CORDON
FIVE for the HANGMAN
January, 1864

The "Chief," Sheriff Henry Plummer, and his two deputies were no longer in power; their execution was the beginning of the long-denied freedom for the people of Bannack and Alder Gulch. In his book, *Vigilante Days & Ways,* Langford wrote, *"The dark shadow of crime, which had hung like an angry cloud over the Territory, had faded before the omnipresence of Vigilante justice. The very feeling of safety inspired by the change was the strongest security for growth and efficiency of the organization."* The Montana Vigilantes would mete out harsh, but well earned, justice to those remaining gang members before their job would be complete.

A NEW LIFE...for Bannack

Sometime before Plummer was captured and executed, he had given Frank Thompson several large bags of gold. Consulting with Wilbur Sanders and Judge Edgerton, it was agreed it should be sent to Plummer's wife Electa in Iowa. Thompson had the gold forwarded by draft. He never heard from her, had knowledge she received it, or revealed how much the gold was worth.

Frank Thompson also paid $42.50 for a casket in which Plummer was to be buried. Due to the frozen ground, burial was delayed. The stiff bodies of Plummer, Ray and Stinson were removed from the gallows and placed in a small workshop in Bannack. [1]

Plummer's final grave-site was described as being at the foot of Cemetery Hill, just a few yards from the gallows. Many stories have been told about the grave being robbed and Plummer's remains, especially his skull, being put on public display in a local saloon for years. The bar burned and the remains of Plummer were lost. Of interest to some was Plummer's arm where Crawford's rifle ball had lodged in his wrist. Reports of the ball being worn smooth and shiny from rubbing in his hand as a fulcrum must have come from the grave robber... purported to have been a doctor from Bannack...very possibly the same doctor who performed the operation on Plummer's gunshot wound, ten months earlier.

WAGNER...testimony after the fact

In Bannack, the task of carrying out the penalty against "Dutch" John Wagner remained. He was taken to the small workshop where a body was awaiting burial. He recognized the frozen body laid out on the workbench as Henry Plummer and said, *"That is the man who got me into all this trouble. Had I never seen him I might have lived an honest man."*

Before execution, Wagner, a German immigrant, requested someone write a letter to his mother in New York. Not satisfied with what was written, he removed the bandages from his frostbitten, bleeding hands and wrote the letter himself. In the letter he told of his crimes and robbery and admitted his sentence was deserved. He consoled his thoughts to dying and asked the hangman, *"How long will it take me to die? I have never seen a man hanged."* He was told by the Vigilante preparing the rope, *"It will be short, John...very short!"* He was hung from the rafters of that small workshop in Bannack on January 11, 1864. [2] [3]

VIGILANTE SHOT...first and only

Not on the list in "Red" Yeager's confession, but certainly on the mind of the townspeople of Bannack, was a Mexican "ne'er-do-well" with an unconfirmed history of robberies and murders from California to the Rockies...José Pizanthia. Several local members of the Bannack Vigilantes decided he had to be confronted. They proceeded to Pizanthia's small log cabin in Yankee Flats, a sloping hillside, south of Bannack. Two members, Smith Ball and George Copley, fear aside, pushed open the door with guns drawn. Ball called out, *"José!...are you in here?"* Ball and Copley got no answer from Pizanthia. They entered the cabin from the bright snow laden outdoors into the dark interior of the cabin. Not being able to see well inside, their answer came in the fiery report of two gunshots. Ball was shot on the hip, but his partner George Copley was hit severely in the chest. They retreated back outside the cabin. Copley, mortally wounded, was carried to the hotel for care. Ball's wound was not life-threatening and he quickly bandaged it with his scarf. Copley, a well-liked citizen of Bannack, died shortly after at the hotel.

When the news arrived that Copley had died, Ball turned angry... others joined and they surrounded the cabin and recklessly volleyed shot after shot into it...but pistols could not penetrate the log cabin. A small mountain howitzer was obtained from Sidney Edgerton's cabin. Several cannon balls were fired into the cabin walls and roof. Pausing, the men surveyed the wreckage of the smoke-filled cabin. Ball saw Pizanthia under a collapsed door and pulled him outside, out of rage, and emptied his pistol into Pizanthia's limp body. A rope was tied around Pizanthia's neck, he was hoisted up and tied to a pole left from the debris of the cabin. They again proceeded to put shot after shot into his dangling dead body. They tore down the rest of the cabin, set it on fire, and threw Pizanthia's body onto the burning wreckage. Many of the men felt such a pyre was too good for someone who had killed their good companion.

After the fire had cooled and died, several women of ill-repute sifted the cabin's ashes for any gold the "Greaser" may have had hidden.

John Lott and Wilbur Sanders, among other Vigilance Committee members, watched the vengeance driven "execution" of Pizanthia with little comment. Sidney Edgerton, who had freely given up the howitzer went to the hillside to watch how it would be used. When the orders were given to tear down the building and burn Pizanthia's body, Edgerton felt it unsuitable of his position to view any more...he left. [4] [5]

ROUNDUP...and corralled

Meanwhile, back in Alder Gulch, the Vigilantes continued their crusade for justice. In the area of some twelve thousand residents there remained six more gang members. Their future was decided secretly by the Vigilance Committee.

One member, Jack Gallagher, sat at a faro table in the "Shades" saloon dealing cards when he looked up and blurted, *"While we are here betting, those Vigilantes are passing a sentence of death on us."* Little did he know how right he was!

Three days after the Plummer execution, the Vigilance Committee met and prepared to set up a cordon around Virginia City with 250 armed men to seal off any and all routes of escape. The members of Plummer's gang, proposed for Vigilante capture were: Jack Gallagher, Boone Helm, Hayes Lyons, Frank Parish, Bill Hunter and "Clubfoot George" Lane.

The word went out to Nevada City, Junction, Summit, Pine Grove and Highland City to muster plenty of armed members and be prepared to stand the test of a cold night. Posses of three men each were assigned to arrest the six "most wanted" gang members.

ARRESTS...begin with six

Frank Parish was the first to be captured and brought before the Committee. He asked, *"What am I arrested for?"* One posse member answered, *"For being a road-agent and thief, and an accessory to numerous robberies and murders...!"* Parish replied, *"I am innocent of all...as innocent as you are."* However, when questioned and confronted with particular facts, Parish confessed. He added an additional robbery of a stage between Bannack and Virginia City to the list, which surprised the Committee.

George Lane was arrested at the store of Dance & Stuart where he worked as a cobbler in his own boot-shop. A small, but strong man, he was hobbled since birth from a deformed foot which forced him to use a cane. When taken before the Committee, Lane also asked "Why?" he had been arrested...and received the same answer as Parish. Lane said, *"If you hang me, you will hang an innocent man."* He was told there was proof of his guilt with, *"... no possibility of a mistake."* Told he would hang, Lane's eyes became moist. He asked if he could talk with a minister. Lane was told he could...and he spent his remaining time, under guard, with the minister.

Meanwhile, the Vigilante cordon, with hundreds of men, closed tighter around Virginia City. One of the six marked for capture, Bill Hunter, tried desperately to avoid the armed pickets. He crawled into a drainage ditch to hide, but suffered severe frostbite from being in the cold, wet ditch. He stealthily made his way out of town and finally reached a ranch and hid under a bed in one of the bunk-houses. He was found by Jack Slade, who warned him the Vigilantes were looking for him and headed to the ranch. Hunter, scared and hurting from the frostbite, struggled and rode off into the Gallatin Valley to hide. [6]

ARRESTED...Jack and Boone

Jack Gallagher and Boone Helm were next to be arrested and brought before the Committee. Boone Helm, one of the most vile and dangerous members of the Plummer gang, was arrested in front of the Virginia Hotel. Three Posse members surprised Helm, told him he was under Vigilante arrest. Two guards grabbed Helm's arms, while a third held a pistol to his head. When brought before the Committee, Helm staunchly sat on a bench, with a bold look of defiance and asked, *"What do you want of me here?"* The committee stated the charges against him in a deliberate and angry tone,...from robbery and fraud, to being a killer. Helm exclaimed, *"Ah! If I'd only had a show, if I'd only known*

what you were after, you would have had a gay old time in taking me."
Helm, staring at the committee, boldly denied everything....that he
would swear to his innocence on the Bible. One was provided and Helm
blatantly swore he was a good man. The committee, disgusted with his
outright lies, told him, *"Your life for many years has been a continuous
career of crime. "... you should die!"* Surprised, Helm looked around and
stated, *"I have dared death in all its forms, and I do not fear to die..."*
and defiantly demanded, *"... give me some whiskey."* He passed the
remainder of his time before the Committee swearing at his captors.

During their search, one of the Vigilante posse members found Jack
Gallagher asleep in a gambling room at the "Shades" saloon. Rolled up
in a blanket, he had a pistol and shotgun by his side, but, surprised by the
posse, he had no chance to use them.

When brought before the Committee, still half-drunk from the night
before, Gallagher laughed and openly talked with Committee members....
he gave little notion to the severe consequences he faced. He helped
Plummer plan, and carry out, stage robberies and helped with the cover-
up of the shooting of Dillingham in Alder Gulch. He asked, *"What is
it all about? This is a pretty break, isn't it?"* When finally informed of
the charges and penalty he faced, Gallagher sat down and began to cry.
Suddenly, he jumped up and asked, *"...who peached on me?"* He was
told, "Red Yeager" and that Red had been hanged. When told he would
face the same fate, he said, *"My God! Must I die this way?"* He shouted
and swore at the Committee as he was taken away to hang.

FLAP JACKS...wasted

Hayes Lyons still remained on the Vigilante "most wanted" list.
The posse knew Lyons frequented the Arbor Restaurant. They entered
and searched the restaurant, but Lyons had already left. He fled across a
rocky ledge overhanging the gulch and made his way back to his cabin.
When the group came upon the cabin the leader pushed open the door to
find Lyons inside, ready to eat some flap-jacks. With his pistol leveled at
Lyons, he called out, *"Throw up your hands!"* Startled, Lyons hurriedly
stuck his hands in the air... and the flap-jacks fell to the floor. Lyons, well
aware of his dire situation, calmly said, *"You disturbed me in the first
meal I have had...in six weeks."* The leader hesitated, but graciously told
him to finish his meal...they would wait. Lyons dejectedly told him he
had lost all desire to eat. *"Will I hang?"* he asked. The leader promised
him nothing, but warned him, *"You had better prepare for the worst."*
Lyons managed a smirk, *"My friends advised me to leave two or three*

days ago." He was then asked, *"Have you heard of the execution of Plummer, Stinson and Ray?"* *"Yes,"* Lyons replied, *"but I don't believe it.!"* The leader scoffed, *"You can bet your sweet life on it."* Lyons heard the Vigilance Committee's charges against him, including the killing of Sheriff Dillingham. He was asked if he had anything to add. Lyons stood erect and said, *"...I am not guilty! I have committed no crimes...I am as innocent as you are!"* Earlier Lyons had actually boasted, in front of witnesses, of taking part in killing Sheriff Dillingham. The Committee declared he would hang for the shooting.

Two more "suspicious characters" were arrested in Highland City during the hunt. When brought before the Committee they were questioned. With no evidence found against them, they were freed.

The search continued and netted the capture of five of the six wanted road-agents. Without any shots being fired no one was killed, although each one of the posse carried plenty of fire power. Guards also mixed into the onlookers to prevent any rescue attempt. Hundreds of volunteers participated in the trap and it proved successful. For some Posse members it was a cold and gruesome night...but nothing that a hot meal and a good shot of "Tan" wouldn't cure.

Many of the volunteer guards used in the trap were disturbed. They had not captured Bill Hunter, who used a drainage ditch to escape. At the questioning of the five other captives, one of the Posse guards, cold, hungry and disgusted, felt they should all pay the ultimate penalty. He called out, *"Hang all of them...Hang 'em on their history!"*

The questioning of the captured fugitives was finished. The Committee found all five guilty and the process of deciding and carrying out their penalty began immediately.

HANGMAN'S HOUSE...next stop

After the Vigilance Committee met and discussed a proper penalty for the five men, the President of the Committee told the five men captured, *"You are now to be taken to the scaffold..."* and hanged! He further asked for "last requests" and gave them the opportunity to confess any crimes they may have committed or had knowledge of. All of the captured gang members were secretive about their past and declined to speak.

The guards began to bind their arms when Jack Gallagher snarled, *"I will not be hung in public!"*... and pulled out a pocket knife, put it to his throat and said, *"I will cut my throat first."* "Cap" Williams pulled his pistol, pushed it into Gallagher's face and said, "If you make another

128

move of your arm, I will shoot you like a dog!" Gallagher knowing Williams would shoot him, gulped, and dropped the knife. Boone Helm watched with disgust and said, *"Don't make a fool of yourself, Jack. There is no use or sense in being afraid to die."* The guards tied the arms of both Boone Helm and Gallagher and led them away.

The procession halted in front of the Virginia Hotel, where "Clubfoot George" saw Judge Dance. He called to him and pleaded for clemency. Judge Dance sorrowfully denied he could help. Rejected, Lane asked, *"Well then, will you pray with me?"* The Judge said, *"Willingly!"* and dropped to one knee. Gallagher joined Lane and the Judge. Lane struggled, but knelt to the ground...while the dismayed guards waited.

Helm was unconcerned about the morbid situation he faced. He turned to Gallagher, and said, *"Jack, give me that coat, you never gave me anything."* Gallagher wore a handsome blue cavalry coat trimmed with beaver fur. He replied gruffly to Helm, *"Damned...little use you'd have for it!"* Helm turned, recognized someone else in the crowd and called out, *"...they've got me this time, got me sure, and no mistake!"*

Hayes Lyons again begged to see his mistress, but the answer was the same... *"No!"* Guards recalled, last summer, the disturbance a woman had caused and freed Lyons of the charge of killing Dillingham...it would not happen again.

A LAST REQUEST...some do, some don't

Final preparations at an unfinished building were complete. Five ropes were hung across a main beam, secured to the log wall of the room and looped into a noose. Dry goods crates were placed for the drop... deemed high enough to break the neck and avoid strangulation. Pull ropes were tied to each of the boxes. Each of the doomed men were led into the building and climbed onto the boxes. The hangman, "X" Beidler, adjusted the noose around each man's neck to assure, hopefully, a quick, painless death.

George Lane faced the door in the front of the building and was positioned at the east wall of the room, with Lyons next to him. Gallagher was positioned in the middle, with Helm on his right. Parish was at the west wall. The committee decided each man should be executed one at a time, starting with George Lane and ending with Lyons. Men were assigned to pull the cords attached to the boxes to spill each man into eternity.

DESPERATE FIVE...face an end

George Lane, the first to hang, saw an old friend among the spectators and sadly called out, *"Good-bye, old fellow, I'm gone."* Not waiting for the guard to pull the box, he jumped...and died quickly without pain. As others watched Lane die and his limp body twisting, Boone Helm quietly and somberly muttered, *"There goes one to Hell."*

After the noose was put over Gallagher's head, he sneered, *"How do I look, boys, with a halter around my neck?"* Beidler retorted, *"Your time is very short!"* He reminded each of the doomed men they could make a last request. Gallagher took the hangman at his word, *"Well then,"* he said, *"I want one more drink of whiskey before I die."* Depravity came over the small crowd of spectators in the building, until an old miner in the crowd barked, *"Give him his liquor!"* A drink was brought, but the noose restrained Gallagher's ability to swallow. He shouted to the hangman, *"Slacken the rope...and let a man take a parting drink..."* Beidler loosened the noose and Gallagher drank his whiskey.

Boone Helm watched Gallagher savor his final drink and felt, he too, should be granted a last request. Angrily, he held his blistered, frostbitten finger into the air and demanded, *"For God's sake, if you're going to hang me, I want you to do it, and get through with it. If not, I want you to tie a bandage on my finger."* His final request was ignored.

As Gallagher watched Lane die, he knew he would be next. The drink had emboldened his spirit and he cursed everyone in the crowd saying, *"...I shall meet you all in the lowest pit of hell."* His diatribe of curses continued, *"I hope that forked lightning will strike every strangling s...of...b's of you!"* The box was yanked from his feet. His body twisted and jerked... and then stopped!

Boone Helm stared hard at the quivering body of Gallagher...as if recalling the past. Helm had faced death before. Caught in a fierce snowstorm in the hills...he resorted to cannibalism. He survived the storm, his companion did not.

Helm looked away from Gallagher's lifeless body, and remorsefully said, *"Kick away, old fellow. My turn comes next. I'll be in hell with you in a minute."* He then shouted loudly, *"Let her rip!"* The drop broke Helm's neck and he joined Gallagher in eternity.

Frank Parish, somber and renounced all the while, requested his scarf be placed over his face. A guard climbed upon the box and tied the scarf over his head, covering his eyes. The box was pulled...and Parish joined the others, quickly without pain.

Hayes Lyons, the last to hang, looked at the still bodies of Lane to his left and Gallagher to his right, and gave up any hope of a reprieve.

Instead, he started making requests...that his mistress be given her watch, which he still carried...that she take care of his burial...and finally, that he not be left hanging for a long time. Beidler shouted the order, and the guard pulled the cord on the drop box. Lyons joined his cohorts in eternity...and into Montana history. [7] [8] [9]

Grave markers of Frank Parish, Jack Gallagher, Boone Helm, "Clubfoot George" Lane and Hayes Lyons at Boot Hill, Virginia City. (Note: Original wood markers are on display at Thompson-Hickman Museum, Virginia City, Montana.)

BOOT HILL...the last stop

Granville Stuart later wrote in his diary, *"All of them said they were innocent, but their guilt appeared well established."* Also written by James Morley in his diary, *"Such wholesale hanging ought to rid the country of these desperadoes who have rendered traveling so dangerous."*

When the hangman, "X" Beidler, later heard comments that the five doomed men appeared fearless and calm facing their ultimate, he asked "Old Man" Clark, a spectator, what he thought about the hanging. Clark emphatically replied, *"They were all cowards at heart. Their courage was whiskey courage, and they were only brave when they had the best of it."* [10]

The five bodies remained on the scaffold for about two hours before they were removed. All were later buried in a solitary knoll on Cemetery Hill, overlooking Virginia City. They were buried in the same order they occupied on the crossbeam in Hangman's House on that cold January day. Simple wooden "headstones" would mark each of their eternal resting place on that lonely knoll, appropriately named, "Boot Hill."

MORE HISTORY...Jack Gallagher

Late in 1863, after the Dillingham shooting, *(See chapter 7)* Jack Gallagher gained austerity in Virginia City as a desperado, but he lacked the courage to fight...unless he surely had the upper-hand.

Earlier, at a bar in Virginia City, a local blacksmith, John Temple, had been shoeing oxen and came in for his afternoon drink with friends. A fight broke out between a pair of canine mongrels. Temple, attempting to relax, tried to break up the fight by kicking one of the dogs, saying to the mutts, *"Here! I don't want you to fight in here!"*

Jack Gallagher boldly interrupted Temple and sternly told him no man should be kicking that dog as if it were his...that he would whip any man that did. Temple, not looking for a fight, but surely not one to back down, looked at Gallagher defiantly and said, *"I'm not going to fight in here; but if you want a fight so bad, come into the street and I'll give you a lay-out! I'll fight you a square fight!"* Temple turned and walked to the door. Gallagher, having no intention of any fighting, saw Temple outlined in the doorway, pulled his pistol and fired, hitting Temple in the wrist. Temple turned and furiously hollered at Gallagher, *"You must do better than that! I can whip you yet!"* Gallagher fired again, wounding Temple in the neck. He approached Temple, about to fire the final shot, when Temple's friends grabbed and stopped him. Temple blurted out, *"Boys carry me somewhere... I don't want to die like a dog in the street."* He survived!

Later at the hanging of Gallagher, Temple, with his arm in a sling, said to the Vigilante hangman, Beidler, *"I wish you had let him run til I got well; I would have settled the job myself!"*

In another instance of Gallagher's bodacious attitude of road-agent dirty work; A Mormon displayed a large amount in green-backs in a Virginia City saloon. Both Gallagher and Hunter followed the Mormon when he left town for Salt Lake City. Days later, they paid for drinks with a suspicious amount of green-backs. Gallagher and Bill Hunter became the prime suspects of robbing and killing the Mormon...he was never seen again.[11]

During the hanging of the infamous five gang members, "X" Beidler had officiated in the adjustment of each man's noose. A group of men gathered to discuss the hanging. One apparent sympathizer for the ruffians asked, *"Well, now, when you came to hang that poor fellow, didn't you sympathize with him, didn't you feel for him?"* Beidler looked disgustedly at the man, answering, *"Yes, I did. I felt for him a little, I felt for his left ear."* [12]

On two historic days in January, 1864, the *Montana Vigilantes* had executed five men, but lost one of their own. In a mere three weeks following the execution of George Ives, the newly formed Vigilance Committee had hanged the gang's leader, Henry Plummer, and had crushed the mainstay of his gang of "Innocents."

Chapter Notes

Note 1. The loops of the hangman's noose are placed behind the left ear for best position to snap the neck, and sever the spinal cord, to justify a swift death.

Note 2. George French, a cabinet maker in Bannack, made the casket Henry Plummer was buried in after being hanged. His son, Anthony French, kept the receipt for the casket in the family until it was later transferred into the archives of the Montana Historical Society, where it remains today. In an article in the *Montana Standard* of August 8, 1954, it was stated Plummer, a frequent visitor to the French residence, was always a "perfect gentleman." (The Pick and Shovel - Sons and Daughters of Montana Pioneers Newsletter.)

Note 3. It was a cold and cloudy day in January of 1864, a day of Vigilante history in Montana. In Virginia City an unfinished building was selected as the "Hangman's House." It would later house the Clayton & Hales Drug Store. The original structure, on the present-day corner of Wallace and Van Buren Streets, is yet standing and is a tourist attraction. The actual site is open to the public to view where five men were hanged by the Montana Vigilantes to pay for their corrupt actions. (It is believed the "original" interior of the log building may have been refurbished to manage stress of the aged structure).

Note 4. Years later, a past Sheriff was questioned if the bodies of the road-agents were really interred at the sites marked. It provoked a digging up of the grave of George Lane. The Sheriff stated, ". .. go down right here, about three feet, and you will find him." About three feet down a cover of boards over Lane's body was unearthed and the bones of his deformed foot were retrieved, as well as some red underwear.

The bones of Lane's foot are on display in the Thompson-Hickman Museum in Virginia City, as well as the original wooden head boards marking the five graves. Duplicate markers have since been placed over the original grave-sites.

Note 5. The name of "Hayes" Lyons, hanged on January 10, 1864 in Virginia City, has also been spelled "Haze" Lyons, as used on the original wooden grave markers on display at the Virginia City Historical Museum. A duplicate marker on historic "Boot Hill," as well as various writers, have used "Hayes" Lyons.

CHAPTER 17
VIGILANTES begin ROUNDUP
January 15 to February 3, 1864

HANG HIM...or give him a chance

The execution of the five Plummer road agents by the Vigilance Committee gave the people of Alder Gulch and Bannack a welcome feeling of relief. People could converse freely in the marketplace and among friends. The aura of fear of speaking to someone who may have connections to the road-agents...was gone. Citizens, especially the businessmen, felt a new and brighter future was open to them. The few remaining scoundrels of the Plummer gang had scattered...but Vigilante plans for them had been made. Meanwhile, thoughts of robbery still remained in the minds of a few others.

A young twenty year old yielded to the lust of Plummer's past. While boarding at the local hotel he stole a bag of gold from a miner who slept in a bunk above him. When he tried to trade an unusual shaped nugget, it was recognized. The youth was arrested and brought before the Committee, with banishment decreed for the youth. Charles "Charley the Brewer" Beehrer, spoke up at the Vigilante meeting. *"I don't believe in banishment,"* sparked the German gruffly, *"Death is good, but banishment, No! If a man is not good enough to live with us, we had better hang him, not turn him loose on somebody else. This boy should have another chance."* He stated the boy should get a job, work and repay the gold he stole.

The boy reported daily to Mortimer Lott or Beehrer until he repaid his debt to the miner and the community. The youth learned the error of his action. He later moved to Last Chance Gulch in Helena, then to Portland, Oregon, where he became a well-to-do businessman. [1]

ROUNDUP...begins

The Vigilance Committee met regularly and discussed the verdict and fate of the remaining members of Plummer's gang still on the loose. On January 15, 1864, twenty-one men were assigned the task of rounding up and bringing those members to justice. On the ride north through the Big Hole River area, a small Vigilante posse was sent to find Steve Marshland, thought to be hiding in the area.

In the evening the posse came upon a lonely cabin at the Clark ranch. The posse made camp, built a fire and prepared to rest. Meanwhile the posse leader knocked at the door of a nearby cabin, but there was no response. He cautiously entered and surprisingly found Marshland lying in the bed. *"Are you sick?"* he asked. Marshland weakly replied, *"Yes, I froze my feet while prospecting at the head of Rattlesnake Creek."* Looking around the room the leader asked, *"Did you raise the color?"* Marshland said, *"No. The water prevented me from going to bed rock."* The leader spotted Marshland's guns, including two double-barreled shotguns. He removed them from easy grasp, then told Marshland if he could walk, he could join them for something to eat.

After eating, Marshland was informed he was under arrest for the Moody wagon train robbery. Marshland was asked to show where he had been shot in the chest, but he denied he had been shot and said, *"My breast is as sound as a dollar."* The Vigilante leader knew he was lying and tore Marshland's shirt open revealing the wound. Marshland had no excuse. The leader said, *"The evidence is satisfactory, we made no mistakes in arresting you. You must die!"* Marshland pleaded, *"For God's sake don't hang me. Let me go..."* His request was sternly denied and told, " We will execute every one of Plummer's band... and we hope to catch them all."

A pole was braced against a corral fence and the noose tied. Marshland pleaded he was too young to die. "You should have thought of it before..." replied the leader. He gave the order and Marshland, on January 16, 1864, paid with his life, for his evil days as a member of Plummer's gang. Before he was buried the posse had to guard Marshland's body...the scent of his frozen feet attracted wolves and made the posse's horses highly skittish.

COTTONWOOD...Bunton and Crowell

The small Vigilante posse met with the main party next morning and continued north toward Cottonwood. They rode double file gaining about sixty miles each day. Each man carried at least one pistol and a rifle or shotgun. The company was divided into messes of five or six men, each having a plentiful supply of precooked or dried food.

At Cottonwood one man was sent to scout the town and its inhabitants. They found the town deserted, except for Bill Bunton and his pal, "Tex" Crowell. They surrounded Bunton's cabin and called for Bunton to come out...no answer. When they started to break the door down, Bunton opened it and the Vigilantes rushed inside. The leader, "Cap" Williams exclaimed, *"Bill, you are my prisoner!"* Bunton resisted and "X" Beidler, with more courage than size, tried to force the much larger Bunton outside, but needed help. Williams grabbed Bunton, tied his arms and shoved him out the door. Crowell was also bound and the two were taken to a nearby cabin and put under guard for the night. The next morning Williams, knowing well of Bunton's guilt, told him, *"If you have any business to attend to, you had better entrust it to someone, we can't be delayed here."* Bunton was taken to Lewis Demorest's corral where the gate posts served as a perfect gallows. A plank was set to form the drop. While adjusting the noose, Bunton angered Biedler, telling him where it should be properly placed... as if Biedler had little experience at the task.

Bunton asked, *"May I jump off myself?"* Biedler replied, *"You can if you wish."* Bunton exclaimed, *"I care no more for hanging than I do for taking a drink of water, but I should like to have my neck broken."* The men were prepared to kick the plank away when he yelled, *"Here goes!"* and Bunton jumped! He died on January 19, 1864.

"Tex" Crowell had been arrested and tried by the men of the posse, but no crimes had been found against him...he was set free. Feeling a strong need to leave, he excitedly climbed on his horse and rode away!

Crowell, actually a spy for Plummer, helped plot the Leroy Southmayd stage robbery. Bill Bunton was instrumental in several Plummer-planned stage holdups, one being the "Bummer Dan" McFadden robbery last October.

HELL GATE...Carter and Skinner

After dark, the Vigilante posse headed to Hell Gate where they suspected Aleck Carter may be hiding. They reached the partially frozen Deer Lodge River, but in an attempt to cross, the ice gave way plunging men and horses into the freezing water. After rescuing the men and horses, they arrived at Jemmy Allen's ranch and spent the night getting warm and drying wet clothes. In the morning they were accompanied by Charles Eaton, who was familiar with the country. Snow drifts, up to two feet deep, slowed the posse's progress. One horse stumbled in a hole, breaking a leg and had to be shot. The horses were accustomed to locating bunch-grass, but they had problems finding any in the deep snow. The posse camped several miles outside of Hell Gate, where they expected to find Carter. A scout was sent to town and when he returned the group swiftly mounted and rode into town.

Cyrus Skinner, as he stood in front of a cabin next to his saloon, was told, *"Throw up your hands."* He was quickly bound as Dan Harding rushed into the cabin and found a man asleep. Cautiously he leveled his pistol at him and hollered, *"Aleck, is that you?"* Half awake Carter replied, *"Yes, What do you want?"* Harding grabbed Carter's pistol and tied his hands before he was fully awake. Unnerved and rather calm about the situation Carter stammered, *"These are rather tight papers . . . ain't they...!"* When told about Marshland and Bunton's execution, as well as the hanging of Plummer in Bannack, he nonchalantly nodded, *"That's all right. Not an innocent man hung yet."*

Skinner and Carter were taken to the Higgins & Worden's store in Hell Gate. Skinner's girlfriend barged into the store hoping to help. She was briskly taken back to her cabin by a posse member, where he found Johnny Cooper. The day before, Cooper had been shot three times by Carter in a quarrel over stolen horses. Cooper, hobbling, was taken back to the store.

During questioning in Hell Gate, Aleck Carter confessed he had helped George Ives when Tbalt was killed, but denied he shot anyone. He also said Tbalt's other two mules were at the Irwin ranch in the Big Hole. Skinner, his bad reputation and character already well known to the group, required no confession. Johnny Cooper was known to have killed a man in Idaho, but escaped before he could be tried. He was believed to be one of Plummer's most valued gang members.

THE BARON.....talks and talks

After questioning, the Vigilantes gained information regarding the location of Bob Zachary. That evening a posse of eight men rode out of Hell Gate and found Zachary at the cabin of "Baron" Barney O'Keefe in the Bitterroot Valley. The "Baron," a flamboyant character wore a Colonel's uniform of the Georgia militia. The Vigilantes arrested both the "Baron" and Zachary, took a knife and revolver from Zachary and tied their hands. Zachary was involved with Ives in the Southmayd robbery, as well as other holdups. On their ride back to Hell Gate the "Baron," unintentionally mentioned a "stranger" had recently stopped at the VanDorn cabin in the Bitterroot Valley. From the brief description, some of the Vigilantes believed the "stranger" to be George Shears, another "wanted" member of Plummer's gang. Three men of the posse set out to arrest him.

When the small posse arrived, their leader Thomas Pitt, asked if this was VanDorn's cabin...it was. Pitt then asked if George was around. *"Yes, he's in the back room."* Shears was taken without any resistance. Walking to the corral with Pitt, Shears pointed out horses he had stolen and said, *"I knew I should have to give up, sometime, but I thought I could run another season."* His complacency to the situation astonished his captors. Pitt said, *"There is no help for you, George. You must suffer the same fate as your companions in crime."* Not knowing his "partners in crime" had been hung...Shears replied, *"I suppose I should be satisfied that it is no worse."* Taken to a barn, a rope was thrown over a beam... Shears started shaking and was told bluntly to climb a ladder. The noose was adjusted, and Shears said, *"Gentlemen, I am not used to this business... Shall I jump off, or slide off?"*

Angered by Shears delay, Pitt told him to jump, *"Alright. Good bye!"* and he jumped! The drop was long and the old, frayed rope unraveled...but survived...George Shears did not. He died on January 24, 1864.

ZACHARY...talks too

Pitt and his two men rejoined the eight man posse and headed back to Hell Gate with Zachary. During conversation between the posse and Zachary, they learned "Whiskey Bill" Graves might be at Fort Owen, also in the Bitterroot Valley.

"Old Man" Clark, with two others, split off to capture Graves. A notorious member of Plummer's gang, "Whiskey Bill," helped cohorts Ives and Zachary in the holdup of the stage carrying Leroy Southmayd. He had openly said that he, *"...would easily shoot any Vigilante"*...that came his way. Clark and his partners were wary and cautious. They met Graves with the stern command to surrender. Backed by pistols, cocked and aimed at his heart, he gave up without a fight...but refused to confess.

He was taken to the nearest tree and a rope was thrown over a strong branch. Clark told Graves to climb up behind him on the horse. With the noose adjusted on Graves neck, Clark shouted, *"Good bye, Bill!"* and dug his spurs into the horse's flank. The horse's sudden leap put the life of a notorious member of Plummer's gang, "Whiskey Bill" Graves, to an abrupt end on January 26, 1864.

HELL GATE....questioning ends

It was January 25, 1864, when the questioning and trial of Cyrus Skinner, Aleck Carter and Johnny Cooper finally ended. Each was condemned to die. Large poles were placed over a corral fence and dry goods boxes placed for the drop. On the way to the corral Skinner broke away, running in the deep snow shouting, *"Shoot . . . Shoot!"* No one raised a pistol. Two men chased Skinner, knocked him into the snow and led him back to the scaffold. With the noose in place "Cap" Williams asked Carter one more time to confess to killing Tbalt. Carter retorted sourly, *"If I had my hands free, you s..o..b..., I'd make you take that back."* To stop Skinner's constant ranting, his pipe was given to him to smoke. He quieted down until the end, but confessed nothing. Both Skinner and Carter claimed as their last words, almost as an allegiance to the dead Plummer, *"I am innocent!"* Without any apparent remorse, both died on the scaffold without pain. Cyrus Skinner, a prisoner with Plummer in San Quentin Prison, had operated the "Elkhorn" saloon in Bannack as a hangout for the gang. Aleck Carter had been more than "just involved" with Ives in the killing of Nicholas Tbalt, he participated in several stage robberies, including the holdup of Leroy Southmayd.

LAST CHANCE...redeemed

The eight man posse arresting Bob Zachary arrived from Hell Gate the next morning. Zachary was taken to Higgins & Worden's store, questioned and found guilty. He asked a letter be written to his mother and family in New York warning them to avoid drinking, card-playing and bad company...three evils that brought him to the gallows. On the scaffold Zachary prayed for the Vigilantes and acknowledged their purpose, *"...God would forgive the Vigilance Committee for what they were doing, as it was the only way to clear the country of road agents."* The rope popped...Zachary died quickly.

Johnny Cooper, because of his wounds had to be brought to the gallows in a sleigh to hang! He asked for his pipe saying, *"I always did enjoy a good smoke."* It was his last...he died without a struggle. [2]

MISSIONS...complete

The twenty one man Vigilante posse had captured and executed eight of the Plummer road-agents and headed back to Alder Gulch. They had fired no shots and none were injured by their captives. They had suffered immensely by the fierce winter weather, some of the worst seen in the area.

They did not return to a hero's welcome, however. Many people felt scorn and mistrust for them. Some historians still write about them with a lack of respect and contempt for their "hurried" action of justice. However, the only "legal" law enforcement officer in the area, Sheriff Plummer, had created his own law to abide by. The citizens rose up against this "bully" and dealt with him as best they knew how. [3] [4]

HUNTER...becomes hunted

The lone remaining road-agent of the Plummer gang, Bill Hunter, was last seen escaping from the cordon the Vigilance Committee placed around Virginia City. Since then he had been reported hiding in the Gallatin Valley. He bummed shelter and food from the settlers as he could.

A group of Vigilantes, posing as roving miners, set out to find Hunter. The posse, led by Adriel Davis, Sheriff of the Junction mining district, had partners John Lott, John Bagg and Richard McLaren. After crossing the mountains between the Passamari (Ruby) River and the Madison River, the group had problems crossing the freezing water and decided to camp for the night. Building a fire, they huddled in their blankets from the cold weather and snow. The following day a mountain snowstorm blew directly into their faces and made travel difficult for both horses and riders.

They still had about twenty miles to the point they had hoped to encounter Hunter. They stopped at the Milk ranch to eat and warm themselves. They continued on, sure they would find Hunter at a lonely cabin in a rocky mountainous area. On Tuesday night, February 2, 1864, Davis knocked at the cabin door and was surprised to find it occupied by three men. He asked for shelter from the storm and welcomed the warm fire. Tired, they placed their guns close by, spread their blankets on the dirt floor by the fire, and were soon asleep. Exhausted and cold from two days riding they slept late.

Getting ready to depart the next morning they casually asked about the loud-snoring man still asleep. Both men didn't know him. He had come two days ago and asked for a place to stay until the storm subsided. Davis and Lott, acted as if he might be a friend, and asked if someone could describe him. The description fit Hunter. Going to the bedside in the cabin Davis shouted, *"Bill Hunter!"* and pulled the blanket back. Startled, Hunter rose up with a pistol in his hand, *"Who's there?"* John Lott poked the barrel of his shotgun in Hunter's face, grabbed his pistol and stood him up. Davis then told him, *"You are arrested as one of Plummer's band of road-agents."* Hunter looked hopelessly at Lott and said, *"I hope you will take me to Virginia City."* Davis said they would.

Outside, Hunter asked if they had a horse for him. Lott pointed to one and said, *"There is the animal you must ride."* Hunter mounted the horse, but the reins were pulled from his hands and he was told, *"If you please, I'll manage these for you. You have only to sit still and ride."*

After a short distance, the group stopped under a lone tree. Hunter realized...he had but minutes left! The group cleared an area, kindled a fire and prepared breakfast. Nervously eating and talking with his captors,

Hunter seemed to forget his fears about what had been planned for him. After eating, a vote among the four Vigilantes was for Hunter's immediate execution. One "nay" vote came from Sheriff Davis, who had told Hunter they would take him to Virginia City.

Davis talked with Hunter and reminded him of the crimes that caused his arrest. He said, *"Of course you know that your offenses...are punished with death. There is no escape for you. We are sorry...sorry for you, but the blame is yours."*

Hunter realized his fate and requested a decent burial. Davis told him the ground was frozen and they had no tools. The sheriff continued, *"... We will inform your friends of your execution, and they will attend to your burial."*

Bill Hunter had qualities to become a hard-working miner, one least likely to harbor the mind-set of one of Plummer's criminals. However, Hunter suffered the same consequences as Plummer...he was promptly hanged! On February 3, 1864, the Vigilantes executed Hunter in the Gallatin Valley, close to present day Three Forks. [5] [6] [7]

Chapter Notes

Note 1. Most gold occurs in a layer of sediment on top of the "bedrock," an impervious layer of rock and clay, which holds the gold. Running water washes the gold free to travel downstream.

Note 2. In less than three weeks the twenty-one man Posse of Vigilantes captured and convicted the remainder of Henry Plummer's gang. Although Plummer's gang had been eliminated, crime continued...and so did the Vigilantes.

Note 3. Sheriff Adriel Davis' quotes (as per Langford) have been edited for clarity.

CHAPTER 18
PART ONE
SLADE meets LANGFORD
Spring, 1863 to March, 1864

STAGE LINE...turns a man mean

In the Overland Stage Line's service most of the "criminalistic" stories of J. A. "Jack" Slade came back to haunt him. Nathanial P. Langford best describes Slade and the problems surrounding Slade's activities in his book, *Vigilante Days and Ways. "People who have once heard of him are prepared to believe any report which connects the name with crime. Wrong as this is on general principles, it has been especially severe in the case of Slade."*

Jack Slade was an honest and amiable citizen, except when he got drunk, then he turned into a whirlwind of terror. He would ride his horse, "old Copperbottom," into saloons and stores, causing utter devastation to customers and store-owners. Sober he was congenial, hardworking, showing no criminal tendencies. When he drank, which became more and more often, he was a raucous rowdy, mindless of what he was doing to his fellow citizens. When drunk, most of the townspeople feared him!

It was Slade's job to control his men of the Overland Stage Line, to make them perform to the utmost. Available personnel were not "pick and choose," it was take what you could get. Riders and drivers were mainly drifters looking for the latest gold strike...hard to find and hard to control. It took a strong, defiant leader to whip dedicated service from these men. At times tempers would sizzle between Slade and his teamsters and angry tales would be embellished to the point where "mean" behavior by the boss would be talked of as "criminal." Slade was a hard man on company thieves, especially when it came to horses, the mainstay of the company's livelihood. Tales were told about his treatment of employees and many times blown out of proportion by an errant trail hand.

BENI and SLADE...shoot out

In the Spring of 1860, Slade was sent to the northeast corner of present day Colorado along the North Platte River to investigate Jules Beni, an Overland station master at Julesberg. A French-Canadian, Beni was thought to be stealing Overland horses and selling them. As station master, Slade had been warned to curb the losses, but they continued.

Slade saw no recourse but to replace Beni as station agent. Whenever Slade and Beni met...they quarreled. Beni hated and swore vengeance on Slade for his demotion.

At a later meeting at the station, Slade was casually talking with an employee. Beni, still working at the station, approached the two and saw Slade was unarmed. Beni drew his pistol and angrily emptied it at Slade, hitting him with all six shots. Seeing Slade still alive Beni ran to his cabin, loaded his shotgun, ran back to the wounded Slade and emptied both barrels into him. Sure Slade would soon die, Beni shouted to his crew, *"When he is dead, you can put him in one of those dry goods boxes and bury him!"* Bleeding and writhing in pain, but still conscious, Slade retorted, *"I shall live long enough to wear one of your ears on my watch guard. You needn't trouble yourself about my burial."*

Immediately after the shooting, superintendent Ben Finklin arrived and arrested Beni. Station hands improvised a scaffold to execute him. A rope was thrown over the scaffold and he was drawn up by the neck several times. Choking and squirming, with his face almost black, Beni promised to leave the country and never come back...he was released. Slade miraculously survived.

An army surgeon from nearby Fort Laramie was called. He removed a handful of lead from Slade's body and attended to his wounds. Soon after attending further treatment in St. Louis, still carrying some of Beni's lead in his body, Slade returned to work and was soon promoted to division agent of Overland Stage Lines.

JULES BENI...returns

Later in the year, Slade learned Jules Beni had broken his promise to leave the area and never return. Slade searched out information to the whereabouts of Beni, suspected to be living at the Cold Springs station in Wyoming. Slade with two friends, armed with shotguns, rode the stage to the station. At the station Beni spotted Slade on the approaching stage and ran. He was quickly captured and tied to a corral fence. Slade, desperately seeking revenge, approached Beni, pulled his Colt cap and ball revolver and recklessly shot him. The ball hit Beni in the mouth, but glanced off his teeth without killing him. At this point, Slade agreed a will should be drawn up for Beni before his imminent death.

After getting pen and paper the will was written, signed and witnessed. Slade casually invited the witness back to the relay station for a drink. Soon he reemerged to stare at the bleeding Beni and snarled, *"Now, you're gonna pay for bushwackin' me in Julesburg!"* He took another drink, set the bottle aside, and slowly poured shot after shot into Beni ...furiously torturing him for the pain he had suffered earlier.

Some accounts say the number of shots over the next hours could not be counted. All at once Slade's anger climaxed and he fired one last shot...more purposeful, killing Beni instantly! He stood back, looked at Beni's limp body and recalled his earlier pledge. He pulled his knife from his belt and cut off Beni's ears!

Slade knew the old Indian trick of cutting off a renegade's ears and sending them to the tribal chief as a warning not to raid any civilian camps. Slade carried Beni's ear...or ears...in his vest pocket, often showed them off, or offered them as payment for a drink.

Following the killing of Jules Beni, Slade returned to Fort Laramie and surrendered to authorities. They declined to take any action in the matter and Slade left a free man. Overland Stage also investigated, but took no action against their employee.

There are several variations written of how Slade killed Beni. However, the question remains; Did Slade cut off one...or both, of Beni's ears? [1]

SLADE...faces a liar

In the summer of 1861, two partners in crime, Henry Bacon and Harry Smith, killed an acquaintance of Slade, P. Bartholomew, leaving his widow with two small children. Both worked at Overland and lived on the Sweetwater River close to Independence Rock, Wyoming. Smith offered the widow a home with him, but was refused.

Bacon and Smith further planned to taunt another wealthy neighbor, Joseph Plante, into an argument where they could kill him and take over his property which included a large, well-stocked store. Plante suspected the plot and contacted Jack Slade, a friend and regular customer. Slade wrote back telling Plante to be careful, protect himself and to have, *"...two rawhide lariats ready."* He would arrive shortly. Slade and four men arrived on Friday with an extra coach.

Slade encountered Smith in Plante's store saying, *"Smith, you said lately that no man could call you a liar and live. Pull out your gun, for I am going to tell you what I think of you, and I expect to be shot!"* Slade put a firm hand on Smith's shoulder, moved close into Smith's face saying, *"You are a liar, a thief and a murderer, and the greatest coward on earth... you killed a man who had two children to support to get his wife. You did not succeed, but I will punish you severely for it!"* Slade

145

pushed Smith away and ordered his men to go to work and tie his arms. The men bound Smith's hands and led him to the corral gateway where Slade looped a lariat over Smith's head, threw the end of the rope over the crossbeam and jerked Smith off the ground, choking him to death. *"Get Bacon!"* Slade ordered. A second rope was tied around Bacon's neck...and he was hoisted into eternity to join Smith. Slade's actions were harsh for "harboring a fugitive." Hanging Smith and Bacon was Slades's form of "trail justice" and it was accepted.

Jack Slade met with Bartholomew's widow and discovered she wanted to go back home. Slade told her to get ready, she could stay with him and his wife until he could sell her dead husband's ranch and stock and secure the money. Slade gave her a free pass on the stage to take her children back home, plus the proceeds from the sale of the ranch and stock. He also gave her the money, about $1,500, from Smith and Bacon's pockets. A few weeks later Slade received a letter from Mrs. Bartholomew's parents thanking him for the help he gave her family. This was one case where Slade's tough form of "trail justice" was quick and gratifying.

GOOD HEART...mean temper

Another case does not prove to be as gratifying. In the late winter of 1861, two Military employees argued...one was shot and killed. The killer, a Mexican, escaped to John Sarah's ranch in Cottonwood Springs. Slade contacted Sarah and ordered him to send the Mexican off his ranch. Sarah denied, saying he was a paying customer. A few nights later a coach loaded with agents of Overland arrived at Sarah's door. A shooting spree erupted shortly, killing Sarah, his Indian wife, an unlucky visitor at Sarah's ranch, plus another old rancher named Lonnel. Two of Sarah's daughters, one of which had a newborn baby, crawled out a back window and escaped the shooting. Frederick Winters, a guest at Sarah's, also escaped. Winters made it to Fort Laramie and gave authorities a report of the shooting. Weeks later the young girls and baby were found in the prairie...dead from exposure!

Slade had not known of any children on the ranch, but a five year old boy, believed to be the son of Sarah, was found alive by Overland's agents and taken to the stage station. Slade and his wife self-adopted the boy, Jemmy, and raised him as their own child. The authorities ruled Slade had attempted to apprehend the Mexican killer...no charges were filed against Slade.

The killing spree of the Mail Agents was acknowledged to be ordered by Slade, as were all of the actions within his division of Overland. Slade was not criminalistic but his punishment of those who cheated the company, or committed theft, sometimes appeared borderline and severe...especially when reported by disgruntled employees. Hence, "stories" of this tough, unforgiving agent of Overland may have grown out of proportion to the actual truth. [2] [3]

Jack Slade, strict about his drivers not drinking, let their use of whiskey lead to his eventual firing. His utter devastation of ransacking a grogshop and bitter harassment to its owner for selling booze to his drivers was viewed by the officials at Fort Halleck as overboard. Slade was arrested and, if not for a negotiated release by Overland, he may have spent time in prison. Officials at the Fort recommended Slade be dismissed. Overland obliged and on November 15, 1862, Slade and Overland parted company.

PART TWO
HERO SLADE
Too Big for His Boots

ALDER GULCH...new home, no credit

Late in the Spring of 1863, Jack Slade, wife Maria and their adopted son Jemmy, moved to Virginia City. Slade purchased 320 acres north and east of Virginia City and would operate a cow ranch in the foothills, selling the milk to customers in Virginia City.

Soon after purchasing land, Slade decided where to build his cabin. Heading into town to purchase the necessary materials for the cabin, Slade met the sawmill owner, Nathaniel P. Langford. He chose what lumber he needed and had his men load it on his wagon. He met Langford and proposed an offer, *"How long credit will you give me with this purchase?"* Langford coolly replied, *"About as long as it takes to weigh the dust."* Slade, taken back, was accustomed to receiving credit without question. Still enthusiastic about the deal, he replied, *"That's played out."* Langford, not in the credit business, told Slade, *"As I can buy for cash only, I must of necessity require immediate payment on all sales."* Slade disdainfully recalled his teamsters to return and unload the lumber. Just arriving in town Slade needed time to pay, but he still needed the lumber to start building. He told Langford, expecting him to finally agree, *"Well, I can't get along without the boards..."* and he turned and told his crew, *"...load them up..."*

The men loaded the lumber and pulled away. Conversation between the two became very tense. Slade pleaded, but Langford still denied credit. Slade had to unload the wagon of lumber a second time. He took a deep breath and looked hopefully at Langford, as if he should certainly allow certain "noteworthy" men some privilege. He said, *"Oh well, I guess you'll let ME have it."* Langford replied with a quizzical tone, *"Certainly not ...!"* Slade retorted, *"Then I guess you don't know who I am."* Langford replied he did not, but it would not make any difference if he did. Slade then asked with an impertinent voice, *"Well, my name is Slade. You must have heard of Slade of the Overland?"* Langford replied, *"Never before."* Tension continued to mount! Slade motioned to several of his men who just came out of a saloon, *"I'm going to have this lumber, that's dead sure! Come boys, load up the wagon!"* A crowd gathered to witness the ongoing conflict between Langford and Slade.

An old friend of Langford's, John Ely, came out of the crowd and asked him to allow Slade to have the lumber...he would see Langford would receive payment. With deep concern, Langford reluctantly agreed. John Ely could see the tension between the two men would grow to a possible disaster.

It was nine years later in Helena, Langford helped a coach driver with a rough team of horses. The teamster recognized Langford and said he was at the sawmill scene working for Slade. He was sure Slade would shoot someone over the lumber. The teamster told Langford his letting Slade have the lumber, probably saved his life. [4]

CAPTAIN SLADE...meets "Cap" Williams

J.A. "Jack" Slade also started a small, but well equipped, freighting business running into the Idaho gold fields. He outfitted a train of neophyte Colorado miners who wanted to head into the eastern portion of Idaho Territory and into Alder Gulch, the area's newest and largest gold camp. Slade's wagon train, from Denver, soon met with another train heading in the same direction and they decided to combine.

The second train was piloted by James Williams. It was decided a vote should be taken of the drivers to choose the leader of the combined train. Slade, however disagreed, saying he would not be bound by the vote...he should be the Captain! Williams, pulled Slade aside and with firm conviction boldly said to him, *"I understand you say no matter who is elected you will still be captain of this outfit. I want to say whoever is elected captain...will be captain."* He then looked directly at Slade, face to face, and said with an unrelenting voice, *"Did you hear what I said?"* Slade had no answer...Williams won the trail-side election. Slade concurred and agreed to serve as Williams' second in command. This encounter earned Williams the nickname, "Cap" or "Captain." [5]

VIRGINIA CITY...flour shortage

In 1863, Slade's small ranch and milk cows at Virginia City prospered. However, a drought in the Midwest affected much of the Northwest territories. From Albuquerque to Virginia City the land was scorched with burnt crops. Dying grassland, stock and wild life, put people in a desperate need of food. Indians were facing starvation and began to attack wagon trains from Salt Lake that carried food and supplies.

The shortage of food affected citizens of Virginia City and surrounding areas. Rivers and streams lacked water. Boats coming up the Missouri River from St. Louis with much needed supplies could not reach their usual drop-off point, Fort Benton. Instead, boats with supplies were unloaded at the Milk River, 200 miles downstream. An extreme shortage of food developed across the area. Teams of Vigilantes were organized to go house to house in search of hoarders of the staple food... flour.

One of the teams, led by a stern and strong built leader, searched the home of Bridget Emerson. She felt indignant when asked how much flour she had, even though she was in the process of baking bread. She showed the leader her three children plus an older girl she was taking care of for neighbors. The leader then asked where her husband was? He was told, *"Dead!"* He was buried in the cemetery on the hill. Satisfied she was not hoarding any flour, he told her, *"She had enough."* She questioned, *"...flour?"* and he answered, *"No...children!"* The Vigilante searcher told the woman he would see that she had the flour she needed, and left. [6]

SLADE...good side...bad side

Jack Slade recognized the turmoil the shortage caused and volunteered to organize the manpower and equipment necessary to direct a supply train 200 miles past Fort Benton on the Missouri River to bring back needed supplies. He would load the supplies, fight off or console any Blackfoot rebels and return to Virginia City.

This job required the experience and natural abilities of Slade....he rose to the task. His success, without losing a man or horse and wagon, saved the town and hundreds of people from hunger! Jack Slade became a hero and true champion of the people! Slade gained the trust and friendship of the citizens of Virginia City and the surrounding area.

Slade enjoyed his ranch, the work involved, and lived without the stress he faced so much in his earlier life at Overland. His enjoyment included a relaxing drink, but his casual drinking soon became...a necessity!

Slade became belligerent and overbearing to his former friends! His escapade of drunken, boisterous actions grew within Virginia City. [7]

Langford wrote in his book, *"The frequent and inexcusable acts of violence committed by Slade made him the terror of the country. His friends warned him of the consequences, but he disregarded their advice, or if possible, behaved the worse for it. All the respect they entertained for Slade when sober, was changed into fear when he was drunk; and rather than offend one so reckless of all civil restraint, they closed and locked their doors at his approach."* [8]

COURTSIDE MANNER...poor

One morning Slade and several friends, including Bill Fairweather, were arrested by Sheriff A. B. Fox after a night of drunkenness and violence on the town. They were taken before Judge Alexander Davis for riding their horses into several bars, breaking glass fixtures, mirrors, windows and beer glasses. Slade would take gold dust scales, throw them through the window onto the boardwalk, then ride to the next bar without paying for drinks, let alone the damage he caused.

Outside Judge Davis' courtroom, Slade turned mad, drew his revolver and said to Fairweather, *"Go in Bill, I'm with you. We'll teach this volunteer court what its law is worth any how!"* Slade boldly grabbed the writ of their arrest from the sheriff's hands, tore it into shreds, threw it on the floor and stomped on it. Both bewildered, the Judge and Sheriff stood and watched Slade's violent actions before he turned and stormed out of the courtroom.

Paris Fouts, Major Brookie, Judge Davis and other members of the Virginia City Council had intervened in Slade's behalf over past months, preventing the Vigilantes from summarily punishing him. But this outburst, pushed his violence to the limit.

During his ruckus, a large number of the Vigilantes had a meeting over Slade's bad behavior. "Cap" Williams, leader of the group and well known to Slade, approached him and said, *"Slade, get your horse at once, and go home, or you will have serious trouble!"* Startled, Slade retorted, *"What do you mean?"* Even though a member of the Vigilante group, Williams told Slade he had no right to ask...only to, *"...remember what I tell you!"* Slade acknowledged Williams' stern and demanding warning and reluctantly decided to go home. However, once on his horse he recognized comrades in the crowd, became emboldened...and heedless to the stout warning from Williams!

Slade, seeking Judge Davis, found him in Paris Fouts' store talking to John Lott. He boldly interrupted saying, *"I hear they are going to arrest me."* The Judge cautioned him, *"Go home Slade, go at once and behave yourself, and you may yet escape."* Slade, not one used to taking orders, pulled a derringer pistol and pointed it at the Judge's head saying, *"You are my prisoner!"* A friend of Slade's, stepped forward and calmed him to the point where he agreed to leave. Slade noted the gathering crowd outside, suddenly realized the volatility of the situation and returned to the store. He doggedly apologized to the Judge for his excited and poor behavior.

Slade then met and talked with "X" Beidler who was aware "Cap" Williams had just left for Nevada City to request support from their Council. The Virginia City Council was reluctant to act against the tenacious Slade. Beidler, hopefully offered another warning to Slade, *"...get your horse and ride home!"* Beidler knew Williams would be riding into town shortly, probably with support from the Nevada City Vigilantes...to arrest Slade.

Within minutes Williams returned with a large posse and rode up Wallace Street to Pfouts' store. Williams entered and arrested the bewildered Slade. It was determined between members of the two councils Slade should be executed!

Slade was bound and taken out the back of Pfouts' store to the Elephant Corral on a gulch road north of Wallace Street. The corral offered two large gate-posts with a log beam at the top, a perfect scaffold. Jack Slade was lifted onto a large packing crate. A rope with hangman's noose was thrown over the cross beam. Slade's wife, Maria, had been sent for, but it would be a long, desperate ride from their ranch into town.

Slade, warned he had little time left, swiftly sobered to his deadly situation. Seeing Judge Davis in the crowd, Slade called to him and hopefully apologized again. He pleaded that his life be spared, not face the gallows! Judge Davis asked council members to banish Slade instead of hanging him...request denied! The Judge disdainfully looked up at Slade, standing on the crate, and replied, *"Mr. Slade, I can only repeat your words. I have no influence, but would gladly do so if I had."*

The crowd became impatient and shouted, *"Time's up!"* The crate was yanked beneath Jack Slade's feet. He died quickly, without pain.

Joseph A. Slade, 33 years old, died at the hands of the Vigilance Committee on March 10, 1864 for his intimidation of the Judge with a gun and his past history of drunken behavior.

"X" Beidler, not wanting Slade's wife to arrive and see him dangling at the end of a rope, took Slade's body down and removed the ropes. Beidler and James Kiskadden carried the body to the Virginia Hotel.

When Maria arrived, her horse lathered and frothing from the twelve mile ride, she shouted in tears and agony, *"You trash! You hung him like an animal. You could at least have shot him like a man!"* Sobbing, she regained her composure and looked at the men surrounding her and asked, *"Why, oh why, did not some of you, a friend of Slade, shoot him down, and not let him suffer to die on the scaffold? I would have done it had I been here. He should never have died by the rope of a hangman. No dog's death should have come to such a man."*

His wife, Maria Virginia Slade, had his body immersed in alcohol, hermetically sealed in a lined coffin and taken to Kiskadden's house on South Van Buren Street. Because of harsh weather, it was not until June could Maria and son Jemmy, board the stage with the coffin and start for the burial in Illinois, Slade's home. But hot weather and deterioration of the body provoked a hurried burial of Slade's body in the cemetery at Salt Lake City, where it remains today.

Later Langford quotes a friend of Slade's, who had written, *"Slade was unquestionably a most useful man...to the stage line, and to the cause of progress in the Far West, and he never was a robber, as some have represented; but after years of contention with desperate men, he became so reckless and regardless of human life that his best friends must concede that he was at times a most dangerous character, and no doubt, by his defiance of the authority and the wholesome discipline of the Vigilantes, brought upon himself the calamity which he suffered."* [9]

Chapter Notes

Note 1. Paris Fouts' store was only two or three doors west on Wallace Street from the now famous "Hangman's House," where only months previous five of Plummer's gang were hanged. (See Chapter 16). The Elephant Corral was located on the SE corner of Cover Street and Van Buren Street, one block north of Wallace Street.

Note 2. In the search for flour in the Virginia City home of Bridget Emerson, it was reported the searcher was James "Cap" Williams, and the older girl in her care was Martha Jane Canarry, the famous (or infamous) "Calamity Jane." (Unverified)

Note 3. Shortly before the roundup and capture of the five of six "most wanted" of Plummer's gang, it was Jack Slade who found Bill Hunter, the sixth "most wanted", hiding on his ranch under a bunk-house bed. Hunter had been the only escapee of the cordon around Virginia City.

Note 4. There is a Charlie Russell sketch in the Montana Historical Society showing Jules Beni tied to a corral fence with Slade firing at him. The above description of the shooting is deemed the most plausible of the many tales written. Slade's knife used on Beni's ear is on display in the Virginia City Museum in Montana. Jules Beni, Slade's nemisis has also been identified, by many writers, as Benoit, Benni, Bene, Reni, Rene, and Remi.

CHAPTER 19
MONTANA.....WHAT'S in a NAME
BANNACK'S LAST HANGING
Spring thru mid-Fall, 1864

VIGILANCE...pushing the limit

The Plummer gang of road agents had seen its demise by the Vigilance Committee. The thoughts and feelings grew that the victorious group had done their job and may be "out of business." However, the gold camps of Bannack and Alder Gulch were still bustling communities with a steady flow of seekers hoping to find a strike to make them rich, but some "ne'er-do-wells" were still not willing to suffer the labor to gain their fortune. They still looked lustily at their neighbor's riches with evil, conniving thoughts on how they too may share the riches of the gold camp. Meanwhile, the Vigilance Committee had little to concern themselves with during the Spring of 1864. They knew "official" territorial law was on its way and would deal with the "lawless!"

MONTANA...a new territory

In March of 1864, Sidney Edgerton traveled to Washington and talked with President Lincoln about the formation of a new Territory east of the Bitterroot Mountains. There was quite a debate in Congress over using "Montana" as the name for the new territory. Some thought an Indian name would be more appropriate...like " Shoshone." However, when told "Shoshone" meant "snake" in the native language the idea was dropped and told "montanus" was actually respectable Latin as well as Spanish. The choice was made...*Montana*...would do nicely. Montana Territory was formed on May 26, 1864.

On June 22, during his return trip, Edgerton received word by telegraph at Salt Lake City the President had appointed him as Governor of the new Montana Territory. On arriving at Bannack, Edgerton immediately named it Capitol of the new Territory. A census was also commissioned and found he would serve some 16,000 constituents. He now had to appoint and fill legal positions locally. Edgerton appointed John Lott as territorial auditor, Gaylord G. Bissell as Justice of the Peace, Neil Howie as sheriff of Madison County and as Madison county commissioner, Edgerton appointed James Fergus.

However, until law could be formulated, approved and enforced... crime and criminals lived on...and the Vigilance Committee still had a job to do.

The Vigilantes had considerably less to do, but when needed, they could be relied upon to confront evil activity. The following episodes give an indication of how they handled, or mishandled, some situations. With the new government and advent of legal law enforcement, their previous hasty course of action became questionable to many of the people. [1] [2]

MURPHY...vs. Brady

In Nevada City, about bedtime on June 14, 1864, "Cap" Williams struggled to fall asleep when he heard two shots not far away. He paid little attention but just after falling asleep he was awakened and told a miner had been shot. Banding together a few men, Williams, still Executive Officer of the Vigilantes, investigated the shooting. Murphy, the wounded miner was conscious and identified the shooter as a feuding enemy of his, James Brady.

Murphy had walked by Brady's saloon that evening on his way home. Brady, tending bar, saw him and asked Jem Kelly for his pistol, then asked him to take care of his saloon. Brady arrived at Murphy's cabin and proceeded to shoot Murphy once through the window, then again through the open doorway. Half drunk and dazed over what he had done, he threw the pistol into the nearby bushes. Williams later searched and retrieved the pistol. Brady, when questioned, confessed to the shooting. Doctors believed Murphy would surely die.

Paris Pfouts, President of the Vigilance committee, gathered about fifty men at Adelphia Hall to hear the evidence. They passed a guilty verdict and ordered Brady's execution. Jem Kelly, as an accomplice, was ordered to receive fifty lashes. After lawyer William Pemberton put his affairs in order, Brady was taken to the east end of town and hanged.

Brady surely shot with intent to kill, but his death was the only one in this incident...Murphy survived! There was widespread opposition to what the Vigilantes had done. Some said they acted, *"Too fast."* Dimsdale wrote, *"Many felt sorry for his (Brady's) fate."* [3]

KELLY...outer limits

Another incident putting the Vigilantes in poor light was the robbery of a shipment of gold by stage to Salt Lake City. In the latter days of August, the report of a theft of approximately $27,000 at Portneuf River Canyon reached Nevada City. Williams and a twenty man posse headed south to an area close to the present-day city of Pocatello, Idaho. Jem Kelly, an accomplice in the Murphy shooting, was also thought to be involved in several petty crimes in the area. Searching the camps, Williams heard Kelly was caught by several California prospectors for stealing horses and they held him at their camp at the Snake River ferry. On the way to the camp the posse came across the body of a man floating in the creek. He had been shot in the back of the head and the body was badly decomposed. Williams determined the killing was no concern of theirs. They buried the body, marked the grave and continued on to the camp of Californians. Arriving at the camp, they arrested and took possession of Kelly. Hearing all the evidence they unanimously condemned him to death for the robbery. When asked if he had anything to say, Kelly repented his use of whiskey. They proceeded to execute Jem Kelly by hanging him on a tree on September 5, 1864.

Kelly's hanging took place in front of several Shoshone Indians who feared such practice. Some Indians, who watched the hanging, became terribly ill, writhing in pain. The chase and execution of Kelly took the Vigilantes far outside their normal operating area. This did not seem to matter to the men or to Williams...they did their job.

Some questions remained unanswered: Was Kelly one of a "pack of robbers" that stole $27,000? Who was the dead man in the creek? What happened to the other robbers?...to the gold? Williams and his men, content their task was complete, returned to Nevada City. [4] [5]

Not long following the hanging of Jem Kelly, newly appointed Madison County Commissioner James Fergus wrote an open letter to the Vigilantes which ordered them to disband. He claimed at first there was justification for their force of law stating, *"Our roads were infested by Highwaymen beyond the reach of our laws. Our own safety required they be eliminated."* However, he stated, *"...that vigilante justice was a very dangerous tool, and should not replace the laws of our country."* [6]

FINAL TEST...whose law

James Redmond reported he was robbed of $700 by his cabin-mate John "Hard Hat" Dolan. At first Dolan denied any act of theft, but soon after, he suddenly left town for Salt Lake City. His sudden departure was enough to persuade the Vigilance Committee of his guilt. Thinking one man could track down Dolan and bring him back, they sent John McGrath. In no time McGrath learned Dolan used an alias, John Coyle, and lived in a small community south of Salt Lake City. An attempt to arrest him was stopped by the local Marshal, who stated McGrath had no legal papers or arrest warrant which gave him legal status to arrest Dolan. However, McGrath found friends, abducted Dolan and brought him back to Nevada City on September 16, 1864.

It was suspected Dolan and Jem Kelly had conspired in the stagecoach robbery at Portneuf River Canyon and Dolan had left for Salt Lake City to collect his share of the loot. A portion of the money Dolan stole from his cabin-mate was recovered. The balance of the robbery was collected by the Committee and returned to Redmond.

Paris Pfouts was astutely aware of the public opinion and conducted, as Dimsdale wrote, *"...a patient and lengthened trial."* They found Dolan guilty and sentenced him to death. Dolan admitted the theft explaining he was drunk and would make restitution if his life was spared. His request for leniency was denied. Knowing there may be overwhelming reaction against the execution, "Cap" Williams called up several men to form an armed sentinel to march Dolan to the gallows. At the site of a butcher's hoist northeast of the town, Williams addressed the large riotous crowd, *"It has been said you will rescue the prisoner."* His booming voice drew silence, *"Don't try it for fear of the consequences."* Dolan spoke his last words admitting the theft and again asked for pity.

The crowd called out to spare Dolan's life. Just before the fatal moment, a guard in the crowd was pushed by an unruly supporter of Dolan. The guard leveled his pistol at him and as he did, the man thrust his hand inside his coat showing the butt of a gun. The guard shouted a warning, *"I say to you sir!"* and pushed his pistol into the man's face, *"Just move your arm a couple of inches or so, will you? I want to hit that big white button on your coat."* The frightened man lost courage, swore, *"Hell!"* and bolted out of the crowd.

The ensuing drop at the gallows and the taught rope plunged Dolan into eternity. Guards in the crowd called out, *"Fall back!"* As the guards' rifle and pistol hammers clicked, the crowd hurriedly left. They rolled over one another and knocked a wagon full of men over in their stampede. No great injury occurred and normalcy slowly returned. The guards marched off and the disappointed crowd dispersed. [7] [8]

R.C. RAWLEY...a drunk no more

During the exorcism of the Plummer regime in Bannack, R. C. Rawley took to the hills and was never heard from until September of 1864. He came back to Bannack, possibly from Colorado and went to work in the neighborhood unnoticed by many. He had previously been associated with Stinson, Lyons and other associates of Plummer. He was not in the forefront and may have been no more than an undercover spy, if anything. Upon return he worked quietly but his visits to town, the saloons and his drunkenness, defied his attempt to remain unnoticed. He had frozen and lost both his feet earlier. A detail of Vigilantes was sent and unobserved, quietly arrested Rawley. There was no pretense of trial. His past history in Bannack with Plummer's gang spoke for his guilt. Townspeople awoke the next morning, October 31, 1864, to find Rawley's body swinging from the gallows in rags... footless and cold.

Amede "Mitty" Bessette, complained of the actions of the Committee, stating Rawley had done nothing but write a letter to complain about his earlier scrape with the Vigilantes. Rawley became the 27th victim to be hung by the Vigilantes, as well as the last execution in Bannack. [9] [10]

Were the Vigilantes popular or hated? Or were they an accepted part of the community and its structure? In his book, *A Decent, Orderly Lynching*, Frederick Allen states, *"The Vigilance Committee remained fully intact and operational, serving as a self-appointed shadow government...."* He further writes, *"A more accurate analysis would be to say that the vigilantes were popular and acted through intimidation, much as they accused their targets of doing. As we have seen, very few settlers criticized the vigilantes even in the privacy of their diaries or letters home."* [11]

Chapter Notes

Note 1. Law and order, legally came in the new territory of Montana, but the robberies and the killing continued. The hard-working citizens were becoming more aware of the former questionable penalties dealt out by the Vigilantes. They deemed something less harsh than hanging for a simple robbery.

Sidney Edgerton, as governor, had a task setting up reliable and trusted enforcement. Commissioner James Fergus openly required legal penalties be applied by established courts for the end of former atrocities by the Vigilantes. There would be no more hangings for minor and indiscriminate robberies and legal trials for all crimes against the public. The "new" Vigilantes tried to maintain law as before, but were looked upon as "copycats" of the "original" Vigilantes and with far less respect!

CHAPTER 20
ORIGINAL LEADERS COMPLAIN
TERRITORIAL LAW - 1864

NEEDED...no more

The originally formed Montana Vigilantes, organized in December, 1863, with Wilbur Sanders as Prosecutor, Paris Pfouts President, John Lott Secretary and James Williams as Executive Officer...were not necessarily the same members and officers of the "new" Vigilante organization that continued in Montana into the 1870's. Their original agenda was to eliminate the killers and robbers associated with Henry Plummer, who had infested the area of Bannack and Alder Gulch. It was not until Plummer's gang of "Innocents" was crushed and Territorial law was formed, did the agenda of the Vigilance Committee change.

Because of the immense area of the new Territory, a law enforcement program was slow in coming. The Vigilantes recognized their need to assist and support law and order. Fear of the "gangs" was gone but individual crime continued. As law enforcement grew and criminal activity diminished, the actions of the "new" Vigilance Committee lost citizens' support. They were looked upon as unnecessary...or ruthless, even criminal!

VIGILANTE FORMATION...true to the order

With Sander's conviction and quick execution of George Ives (less than an hour after his conviction, he was hanged), the citizens could finally envision a crack in the armor of the criminal behavior they had faced for so long. Before they set out to capture Aleck Carter, twenty-four men met in the Lott Brothers' store in Nevada City and hurriedly prepared and signed a document...and their program for *Justice* gained life!

The infestation of criminals and hoodlums from California, Washington and Idaho Territories into the new Territory of Montana was relentless. They fled from the advent of law and order in those territories. Now they would be fleeing from soldiers of justice that would be known in history as the new *"Montana Vigilantes."* The Vigilantes would clear the criminals with strong support from the miners, merchants, ranchers and all of the area citizens. Hundreds of volunteers banded with the newly formed Vigilance Committee.

The Vigilante Posses pursued criminals north to Gold Creek, Fort Owens and all points in between, even as far south as Salt Lake City. They would rout the criminal infestation with the aid and backing of all they met. In less than two months they hanged twenty-one of the most virulent criminals plaguing the area, including Sheriff Henry Plummer in Bannack. Their performance was swift and decisive...so profound as to be copied by others for years to come.

In March, 1864, Congress finally accepted the establishment of the Montana Territory to be carved out between the Idaho and Dakota Territories. Montana had territorial law...and its first Governor... Sidney Edgerton. The new Governor established courts, judges and law enforcement officials. With legal officers appointed to enforce the newly formulated law...the continuance of "Vigilante Justice" seemed unnecessary!

HOSMER...Grand Jury

The Vigilantes had repeatedly been told to quit...to disband...but they did not. Chief Justice Hezekiah Hosmer, in his charge to the Grand Jury on December 5, 1864 said, *"It is no part of the business of this court to find fault with what has been done, but rather, in common with all good citizens, to laud the transactions of the organization, (Vigilantes) which in absence of law assumed the delicate and responsible office of purging society of all offenders against its peace, happiness and safety."* He further claimed the late Henry Plummer as the, *"...greatest villain of them all...with hands reeking with the blood of numerous victims."*

Judge Hosmer continued to plead with the Vigilance Committee to stop. *"Summary executions are no longer necessary. No law abiding citizen wishes their continuance. They should at once and forever be abandoned."* He bluntly added, *"Let us erect no more impromptu scaffolds. Let us inflict no more midnight executions."* He further charged the Grand Jury, if they acted again, with orders to, *"indict the Vigilantes with murder!"*

LIKE IT...or not

Mixed reports were given, both pro and con, on how the Vigilantes reacted to the tirade of the Chief Justice. Members of the Vigilance Committee met with Hosmer after his charge to the Grand Jury to accept and abide by his hopes for the organization to disband. The Vigilantes did quit...for a while. Their absence must have been looked upon by the criminal faction, at least, as a "demise" of the Vigilantes. [1]

It wasn't until June of 1865, that the Vigilantes felt the Territorial courts ability to handle the job of enforcing Territorial law was still lacking...and they rose up again. In the five months from June to mid-November of 1865, after their return, they captured and executed thirteen more criminals! However, it appeared during their time off, the Vigilantes had grown inept...of the men they hanged, five were..."unknown!"

THURMOND...threatened

During the "time-off" period James Thurmond, a defense counsel in the George Ives trial, was banished from the Territory. He went to Utah and in revenge started to file civil charges against any Vigilante member who came through the area. Governor Edgerton sent Wilbur Sanders with a letter to the Governor of Utah asking that Thurmond be told to desist his civil suits. The Vigilantes also cautioned Thurmond to quit his ranting, or he would be brought back to Montana...and hanged! The threat worked!

In September, 1865, Governor Edgerton returned to his home in Tallmadge, Ohio worried about his ability to raise children properly in Montana's vast new Territory. Newly elected President Andrew Johnson filled the position of Territorial Secretary with an Irish exile, Thomas Francis Meagher, who had been banished from the land of his birth for acts against the British. He petitioned President Johnson for a position in the new Territory and accepted the position as Secretary. He would later serve as acting-Governor while Edgerton pondered his return to Montana. President Johnson later urged Edgerton to resign and appointed a Kentucky Democrat, Green Clay Smith, as Governor of Montana Territory. Meanwhile, Montana's original population of 16,000 would grow with an influx to new found gold strikes. The telegraph would come to Montana in 1866, opening connections to the east and a flood of citizens.

In September of 1865, Thomas Dimsdale a staunch supporter of the Vigilantes, succumbed to his chronic illness. His successor, as editor to the *Montana Post*, Henry Nichols Blake, a Boston lawyer was immediately notified he had been "elected" into the Vigilantes organization.

In 1867, Dimsdale's book, *Vigilantes of Montana*, was first printed publicizing the Vigilantes actions over the years. Dimsdale's book emboldened the formation of the Vigilantes and helped endow the public with a sense of security not seen since the end of Plummer's reign of plunder. [2]

VIGILANTES...return of justice

Seven more hangings would take place in the first five months of 1866, one of which was brought about by the acting-Governor Meagher. In November, 1865, a drifter, J. B. Daniels, stabbed a man in a Helena barroom brawl. He was captured and convicted of manslaughter. His friends petitioned for a release and stated the case was clearly self-defense. Acting Governor Meagher, moved by a fellow Irishman, signed Daniels' pardon. Justice Lyman Munson disagreed, stating Meagher was "drunk" when he signed the pardon. Daniels was released and promptly threatened some of the jurors in his conviction. Knowing of the Vigilante interest in the case, he asked to be taken back into custody for fear of his life. However, the Vigilantes captured Daniels and promptly lynched him on the famous "Hanging tree" outside Helena. With all the pardon-bickering between Meagher, Munson and the lawyers of the case...the Vigilantes would show they still had the upper hand!

HOSMER...second request

In August of 1866, at the behest of several lawyers in the area, Chief Justice Hosmer gave a second charge to the Grand Jury. Most of his speech, which praised the Vigilantes, could have been written by now-deceased Dimsdale.

Hosmer seemed to break ranks when he said, *"From frequent conversations with influential members of the Vigilantes, who understand the unfavorable tendencies of their society, I learn that as soon as they can feel assured that the Courts and Juries will meet the demands of society, they will freely disband."* Again the Vigilante Committee vowed to support the Courts...but, did not disband.

In December of 1866, it took the killing of five men in a claim-jumping shootout at Cave Gulch, northeast of Helena, for the Vigilantes to decide upon a new approach...to openly threaten hoodlums and criminals. The Helena Vigilante "Committee of Safety" posted "warning" signs saying, *"Read and Reflect,"* and continued to state crime in the recent past had again risen too much for the citizenry and threatened, *"Therefore, this is to notify all whom it may concern, that crime must and will be suppressed; and to that end, all offenders will be summarily dealt with, and punished as of old* (hanging). *By order of the Vigilance Committee."* [3]

After only two months on the job Governor Smith, not impressed with Montana's desolate mountainous country, decided he could better perform lobbying for the new Territory in the nation's capitol. His move would elevate Meagher back into the position of acting-Governor. The political bickering did little for the formation of a workable law-enforcement program. The Vigilantes would remain the major force in keeping the peace.

VIGILANCE COMMITTEE...discontent

Older members of the hierarchy of the original Montana Vigilantes could see problems brewing...indiscriminate hanging of mere thieves and pick-pockets by the new group of "Vigilantes!" The hanging of a thief in Nevada City, who had already been convicted and originally banished, struck discord with the elders. In early March of 1867, in Highland City near Butte, the core of the original Vigilantes posted the following:

Notice!
We, now, as a sworn band of law-abiding citizens, do solemnly swear that the first man that is hung by the Vigilantes of this place, we will retaliate five for one, unless it be done in broad daylight so that all may know what it is for. We are all well satisfied that, in times past, you did do some glorious work, but the time has come when law should be enforced.
Old fellow-members, the time is not like it was.
We had good men with us; but, now there is a great change. There is not a thief that comes to this country but what "rings" himself into the present committee. We know you all.
You must not think you can do as you please.
We are American citizens, and you shall not drive, and hang, whom you please.
{Signed } Five for One

Because the leadership of the new Vigilante Committee was wrapped in the secrecy of their by-laws and membership in the Masonic Lodge, it is difficult to determine when any change took place and how it affected some of their leaders.

Paris Pfouts, the President of the original group, left Virginia City in 1867, returned home to St. Louis. He never came back.

Wilbur Sanders, a steadfast supporter of the Vigilantes, became deeply involved with the politics of the new Territory. He created a leading law partnership and acted as President of the Montana Historical Society from its inception in 1865 until 1889.

James "Cap" Williams retired from the Vigilantes in 1867 and returned to run his stable in Nevada City. He had married a persistent, nagging woman in 1866, bought a small ranch and fathered seven children. He ran into financial difficulty and lost his cattle twice, once due to a bad loan, and once due to a bad winter storm in 1887. During the storm he quietly walked into a pasture ...and committed suicide by drinking a bottle of Laudanum.

John "X" Beidler moved to Helena and still served as a Vigilante. He formed the "Committee of Safety," and became a Deputy Marshal. Not being good at saving money, he died broke in 1890.

Nathaniel Langford, an avid supporter of the Vigilance Committee and writer of the book, *"Vigilante Days and Ways,"* was approached to become the "Chief" of the Vigilante movement, but declined. In 1868 he was appointed by President Johnson to become Territorial Governor, but the Senate declined confirmation and the appointment died. In 1872, after diligent lobbying to have a National Park designated, he was appointed to be Yellowstone National Park's first Superintendent. (See Addendum; "Langford").

AGENDA...complete

The original "Montana Vigilantes" had a demanding agenda forced upon them but they accepted the challenge. In a short forty-two days they completed the job...Henry Plummer and his associates became part of Montana's historical past. With success came heralded plaudits for the Montana Vigilantes...they were looked upon favorably by their neighbors. Admiration grew and their ranks were no longer in dire need for replacements.

An excerpt from W. F. Sanders scrapbook stated: *"The good people were all with us. None of them feared us; none of them had reason to fear our midnight visits. There was no law in the Territory when we came together for self-preservation. We did unpleasant work with hands that never trembled. We made it possible for the peaceable to live in Montana, and for the industrious to accumulate and enjoy the fruits of industry. Just as fast as the consolidation of society rendered operative the ordinary processes of law, we retired. While its administration was still feeble or imperfect, we supplemented it. We made civil law respected, and when it came to full power, we bowed to it and went out of business."* [4]

The original Vigilantes executed the greater part of their captured criminals. However, the "new" Vigilantes still carried out their own form of justice, even though Territorial law enforcement would be deemed the standard, enforceable law. By April 30, 1870, they were hanging "minor" criminals with an overbearing attitude, which disturbed the public, the Territorial courts and the "original" Vigilante members. The "new" organization drew harsh criticism.

COPYCATS...no connection

The hangings carried out by the new Vigilantes in the eastern plains of the new Territory and some of the later gold fields, such as Helena, also became unlawful...but possibly justifiable...to them! Newly formed laws were on the books, but in the sparsely populated eastern plains of Montana they lacked enforcement.

Those who felt enforcement was necessary, such as Granville Stuart and James Fergus of the famous, or infamous "Stuart's Stranglers," took it upon themselves to copy the actions of the Montana Vigilantes by hanging cattle-rustlers. They became a scourge on the cattle-rustlers and thieves in the area. Their actions, though unlawful, were not prosecuted.

There were many "wannabe copycats" that acted as captors and executioners of criminals, or "possible" criminals, in and out of the Territory for many years after. They are not to be confused with, or taken as a part of the original Montana Vigilantes or the Vigilance Committee formed by Colonel Sanders, following his trial of George Ives in December, 1863.

The original Montana Vigilante hierarchy had drifted back to their families and professions. Soon they were replaced by "wannabes" and "copycats"...who sought to confine criminal activity, but lacked the legal form of Justice. The "New Vigilantes" carried on until the 1880's. They were ruthless and hard on crime, but they had taken on a task where kindness was not a reward. They felt they were fighting a just cause and doing good...even though considered unjust and lawless by some...then and yet today!

EPILOGUE
QUOTES on VIGILANTE JUSTICE

NO CSI (Crime Scene Investigators)...in Bannack

With the fight between Henry Plummer and the Vigilantes of
Montana comes the question of who followed the law in this new
Territory. Some writers of history, those "players" who lived during the
1860's, recognized the conquest of the gold fields by a criminal faction.
The pioneers had no legal way, no law or sheriff, to control or eliminate
it! Many pioneer victims sought out known "Brothers" of the Masonic
Lodge, or were members themselves, and they banded together. They
desperately needed to find a way to cope with the rampant crime they
faced...and indeed they did! Secrecy of the Lodge may still, some 150
years later, hide many of the heroes of the 1860's.

Some writers still claim Henry Plummer was "innocent" and that
the Vigilantes were the corrupt party. Delving into many of the Montana
annals dealing with the Plummer era and the passage of over 145 years,
more pieces of history will bring light to the facts...making that theory
hard to believe! History points to Henry Plummer as wearing a "black
hat"...always being the bad guy!

It is hard to recall any writer depicting Plummer as innocent. The
writings of Nathaniel Langford, Professor Dimsdale, Frank Thompson
and Edwin Purple, all who lived in the same era, bear this out. There
is nothing about the "leader of lust" ever attending Thompson's Choir
practice, or going to church services as a member on a regular, or even a
part-time basis. He was, however, a regular at the saloons, brothels and
dance halls. He piloted a gang of killers and robbers to collect wealth
from those on the road but his church donations were seldom, if ever,
mentioned.

One of the most revealing events of the time was the trial of George
Ives for the killing of young Nicholas Tbalt with Wilbur F. Sanders as
prosecutor. Sanders, a lawyer from Ohio was a neophyte to the "miner's
jury" form of justice in 1863. The howl from the countryside for a
conviction was loud and clear. There were only two witnesses, who were
at best...poor!

Others who came forward, however, gave testimony about George
Ives' treatment of them or what they had seen Ives do to others. That
included the remorseless killing of an innocent rancher, where he left the
body in the road, and rode away with his horse. But, that testimony did
not pertain to the killing of Nicholas Tbalt...and Ives could go free on

a lack of evidence. If that happened Sanders could envision himself as Ives' next victim...he had to win!

Sanders could feel the crowd's anger towards Ives...his past history of criminal behavior disturbed them. He felt, by using that history, he could gain enough anger to sway the two "advisory" juries to accept that his "lame" witnesses told the truth.

Sanders determination later helped the Vigilance Committee in their forty-two day roundup and execution of Plummer's gang. They would look at the facts about each gang member's past "history" of crime and illicit behavior, judge them and if warranted, hang them!

The writers who claim Plummer as righteous and nonevil are saying so looking at his actions of 145 years ago and bringing them forward to our time...to our present form of law and today's court requirements for a conviction.

No, history does not record all of the details of Henry Plummer. There is no record of Plummer's connection with George Ives or Buck Stinson, or all the holdups and clear-cut killings the people of Bannack and Alder Gulch had to face. However, the Rattlesnake ranch, supposedly owned by Henry Plummer, harbored little else than roughs, ne'er-do-wells and drifters, all well known and accepted by Plummer. Deer Lodge rancher Conrad Kohrs, on his many trips to Bannack and Virginia City, wrote that he took special care to avoid the Rattlesnake ranch and its "friendly" occupants.

Today the use of fingerprints, DNA evidence, matching gun grooves and casings and first hand testimony...all did not exist in the era of the 1860's during the Vigilantes vs. Henry Plummer. There was barely a law of ethics then...it was the law of survival that emerged and no court or judge ignores or excludes that law!

One writer claims Plummer should never have been convicted in the John Vedder killing. He was tried for the shooting twice...and convicted twice! However, when they write about it they leave out some of the damning evidence. Evidence, such as the Doctor's report, stated the shots entered Vedder's body from above him, most likely from the top of the backstairs...outside the house...not from a position level with him as in the kitchen. This is supported by a witness at the crime scene who stated the flash of the gunshot was downward. If the shooting took place indoors, the witness most likely would not have seen the gun flash and this contradicts Lucy Vedder's testimony.

Let the writer...or reader...appealing to the "good-guy Plummer" scenario take a good look at his "history." Plummer comes to Montana with blood on his hands and adds to the list shortly after arriving.

Plummer would have been charged with murder in the killing of Jack Cleveland in Bannack, either in the 1860's or in today's court. *(see Chapter 6)*.

When Cleveland was shot he was drunk, boisterous and threatened Perkins, who owed him money...not Plummer. It is true Plummer was exonerated in the Cleveland shooting because of what he told the jury. If Cleveland was pursuing Plummer for killing his brother, as Plummer implied in his Bannack "trial," Cleveland could have easily shot Plummer on their way from Sun River and left his body in a ravine for the wolves. Plummer would then have been on Dimsdale's list of "102"!

SLADE EXECUTION...over the line

Talks of forming a new Montana Territory were underway in the Capitol, with its own Justice system; courts, judges, peace officers and laws to govern the citizenry. With the hanging of Jack Slade the question arose...were the Vigilantes getting out of line?

Jack Slade was not a criminalistic personality. He was once a hero to many people; drivers, passengers and support employees of the Overland Stage Line. Slade ruled his portion of the Stage Line with a stern hand, dealing harsh and unforgiving justice to offenders, sometimes death...that was his job!

After being fired from Overland and his subsequent move to Virginia City, he carried with him his own death warrant; his personality! He was friendly, aggressive and out-going, all typically necessary for his position as division agent with Overland. But when he carried his bossy attitude into his private life, it rankled neighbors. (See Chapter18). With a new lifestyle Slade had more time on his hands, which lead him to incessant drinking. Naturally aggressive, bossy and outgoing, Slade became utterly obnoxious when he was drunk. Although his growing drunken behavior and overbearing attitude were not criminal, they brought to bear on the minds of the townspeople an echo of the past problems they saw in killer George Ives! New members of the Vigilance Committee were not willing to subrogate Slade's "similar" actions to the back-burner. The cost could be too great.

After a night of drunken behavior with a friend, Slade was arrested. This belligerent attitude brought the combined councils of Virginia City and Nevada City to have Slade punished. When Slade became sober, he apologized to Judge Davis, who intervened to have the punishment of execution remanded to banishment...but, to no avail. Slade paid the ultimate price of the era...he was hanged.

VIGILANTE...true or wannabe

The enthusiasm for the true Montana Vigilantes waned following the regrettable execution of Slade. With or without enforced law, as many as thirty more hangings continued into the 1870's, mainly in the newer gold camps and into the cattle range prairies east of the Rocky Mountains of Montana.

Following the execution of George Ives, the ensuing *forty-two day Vigilante Crusade* crushed Henry Plummer and the *gang of Innocents*. The once "organized" threat to citizens was virtually non-existent. This left individual criminals and their acts of violence and robbery in the gold camps, plus the growth of cattle-rustlers for the *new Vigilantes* to contend with. Many Vigilante members returned home and their group declined. The new form of criminal activity, for the newly formed, organized Vigilantes to combat, would be the growing thievery by cattle-rustlers in the eastern plains of Montana Territory.

New groups of Vigilante members formed, but with questionable organization, and with questionable members. Possibly they were copycats or wannabes, but not necessarily Masonic members as were many of the original, "scripted" Vigilantes. Some of the *original* members, who felt they were still needed, formed with *new* "do-gooder" Vigilantes to counter the violence. This action gave "license" to anyone... to act as a "Vigilante" against criminal behavior...and to a century and a half of wrath from historians, writers, readers and the general public, who questioned the actions of the *true heroes* of the *original Montana Vigilantes!*

For someone to believe Henry Plummer wore a white hat is entirely their interpretation of history, some 145 years past tense, however...but it is their right to do so.

The Vigilantes of Montana became historically triumphant during the Gold Rush days of the 1850's and 60's. Some of the group leaders became known through the years, but because of their ruthless, sometimes deadly, crusade against the killers and robbers of citizen's golden rewards, their place in Montana history became questionable... their names became hidden. Most of the heroic members of the Vigilantes, to this day 150 years later, still remain unknown in the annals of Montana History!

Recent reports have been heard to say the newer leaders of the Masonic Lodge may delve into their Ledgers and release some long hidden heroes names of Montana History.

In addition, it should be noted, those people who served the Vigilantes were volunteers...they were prospectors, miners, shopkeepers,

172

ranchers...and they did what they felt was necessary, without pay, to rid their society of the plague of lawless criminals.

The Vigilante crusade was not perfect...it just got the job done. In reading some of the memoirs and diaries of those who lived through that era, one can see they were satisfied.

HISTORICAL QUOTES...on Vigilante Justice

"I don't think they made a mistake in hanging anybody." [1]

"The men seized by the committee were not viewed as defendants to be charged with specific crimes and tried by the rule of law, but as menaces to be expunged for the benefit of public order. Their executions were carried out publicly to make a point." [2]

"Far from the control of any organized government the people felt compelled in their might to rise and show the gamblers, robbers, and murderers that they could no longer terrorize the people." [3]

"All of them said they were innocent, but their guilt appeared well established."

Granville Stuart Diary

"...the settlers of Bannack and Alder Gulch express a nearly unanimous sense of relief that the vigilantes were acting to make the trails safe."

From letters and Journal entries of the time.

"Such wholesale hanging ought to rid the country of these desperadoes who have rendered traveling so dangerous."

James Morley diary.

"I hope the (Vigilance) Committee will not have to hang any more men here for I do not like such excitement," she wrote her family, *"but I shall feel Mr. Edgerton will go much more safely now, than he would have gone two weeks ago, for I have no doubt that they intended to rob him..."*

Letter to home from Mary Edgerton, wife of Sidney Edgerton. [4]

In 1884, Granville Stuart, who had met Henry Plummer earlier and repaired his gun in Gold Creek, led "Stuart's Stranglers" into the central plains of Montana with fellow cattlemen, chased suspected horse-rustlers and either shot or hanged thirteen of them along the Musselshell River. Stuart's partner in the roundup, James Fergus, later applauded their campaign, stating;

"The Vigilantes in all their time never did a braver, nobler, or more necessary act or one that paid better in its results." [5]

Even Teddy Roosevelt in 1915, at the birth of WWI, used an anthology: *"Before there was law in California and Montana,"* he wrote, *"and indeed as a requisite of bringing peace there, Vigilantes had to be organized and had to hang people...."* [6]

WAR IS DECLARED!
Vigilance Committees of Alder Gulch and Bannack vs. Henry Plummer Gang.

This may have been one of the headlines of the Montana Post, written by Professor Thomas Dimsdale in early January of 1864, because that's what it was...a WAR! Those citizens who were being ravaged by the pillaging of the robbers and killers took a stand...to fight!

A volunteer army of unpaid warriors sought to protect their rights... their right to work and earn...and to keep what wealth their toils provided!

Their delegations met to discuss, verify and name those who have caused fear within their communities...and to sentence those deemed guilty to a prompt and proper justice!

The only penalty will be...DEATH!
The Vigilantes swept out across the countryside in the dead of one of the worst winters known to southwest Montana. They sought hundreds named by the Vigilance Committee and as their devotion rose, so did their courage. The fear in the ruthless hearts of their adversaries also began to rise!

The war waged was short of any since, but left marks in Montana history bolder and stronger than most. Today many still claim the Vigilantes of Montana were not functioning under law. However, they had a rule of law we all maintain is legally just when necessary...the law of survival!

Dimsdale had reported in his book, 102 murders had taken place, saying they were documented. However, he had probably seen or reported too many to count them with precision. In his book he writes, as others did, of the heroism of those men who cleansed the area, and it is with true regard his entry of those heros is rewritten here:

Montana is saved and they saved it!

"On looking back at the dreadful state of society which necessitated the organization of the Vigilantes, and on reading these pages, many will learn for the first time the deep debt of gratitude which they owe to that just and equitable body of self-denying and gallant men. It was a dreadful and disgusting duty that devolved upon them; but it was a duty, and they did it. Far less worthy actions have been rewarded by the thanks of Congress, and medals glitter on many a bosom, whose owner won them lying flat behind a hillock, out of range of the enemy's fire. The Vigilantes, for the sake of their country, encountered popular dislike, the envenomed hatred of the bad, and the cold toleration of some of the unwise good. Their lives they held in their hands. 'All's well that ends well.' Montana is saved, and they saved it, earning the blessings of future generations, whether they receive them or not." [7]
Professor Thomas J. Dimsdale

"Men of criminal instincts were cowed before the majesty of an outraged people's wrath, and the very thought of crime became a terror to them. Young men who had learned to believe that the roughs were destined to rule, and who, under the influence of that guilty faith, were fast drifting into crime, shrank appalled before the thorough work of the Vigilantes." [8]
Nathaniel P. Langford

Chief Justice H. L. Hosmer in his charge to the first grand jury organized in Montana, December 5, 1864, said;

"Gentlemen of the Jury: The assemblage of a grand jury in this new Territory affords an opportunity for a casual survey of the interests committed to its charge. The cause of justice hitherto deprived of the intervention of regularly organized courts, has been temporarily subserved by voluntary tribunals of the people, partaking more of the nature of self-defense than the comprehensive principles of the common law. It is no part of the business of this court to find fault with what has been done, but rather in common with all good citizens to laud the transactions of an organization which in the absence of law, assumed the delicate and responsible office of purging society of all offenders against its peace, happiness, and safety." [9]

ADDENDUM
PORTRAITS of PLACES and PLAYERS
Historic Sites

Montana Territory.....the home of history

In April, 1803, President Johnson purchased the Louisiana Territory from France. On May 26, 1864, President Lincoln signed the Organic Act, and the new Montana Territory was formed out of the existing Idaho Territory, which was previously part of the Nebraska and Dakota Territories. It included that portion of the Idaho Territory west of the Continental Divide and east of the Bitterroot Range. On November 8, 1889 Montana became a U. S. State.

Bannack.....died and reborn

In the 1860's the discovery of gold on the Nez Perce Reservation brought a major onslaught of miners to the area. Gold fever rose and the search was on in every valley of the Northwest. On July 28, 1862, one group led by John White stopped by a creek, named earlier as Willards Creek by the Lewis and Clark expedition in 1805, where gold was discovered. It was a major strike and soon attracted not only miners, but businessmen hoping make a living providing supplies and equipment to the miners. Hence a town was born and founded in 1862. It was named after the Bannock Indians of the area, but was errantly misspelled as Bannack.

On May 26, 1864, when Montana became a territory, Bannack served as the capital of the Territory, but only briefly, then it was moved to Virginia City. Bannack remained a mining town, with a dwindling population, until it became deserted. Many historic log buildings remain, some preserved and many have been restored. The original buildings were not built to last 140 years into history.

Among the town's founders was Dr. Erastus D. Leavitt, a physician. He gave up his medical profession to become a gold miner. Dr. Leavitt arrived in Bannack in1862 and practiced both medicine and mining gold. He soon found he had a greater reputation as a physician than as a miner. Subsequently he moved to Butte, Montana, where he devoted the rest of his life to his medical practice.

As part of the Bannack State Park, the site of the present "ghost town" was declared a National Historic landmark in 1961.

Virginia City...tobacco money

In May of 1863, six prospectors stopped by a small stream to rest. They were tired and ragged from their search for gold and being unduly taunted by warriors of the Crow Indians. They knew they were close to Bannack, where they had started. While others of their party went upstream prospecting for enough gold to hopefully buy some tobacco in town, Bill Fairweather and Henry Edgar remained to set up and tend to the camp. They had spotted an exposed layer of bedrock in the nearby creek, heavily lined with Alder trees. They wistfully panned the stream and struck enough gold, not only to buy their tobacco...but it turned out to be the richest gold discovery of the country.

The site where Virginia City would be built, was part of the Dakota Territory until March when it became part of the newly formed Idaho Territory. In May of 1864, it became part of the Montana Territory. Shortly after, Virginia City, with a growing population, became the second capital of the new Territory. It is now the County seat of Madison County and in 1961 also became a National Historic Landmark District.

Lewiston, Idaho

Lewiston is located at the confluence of the Snake River and the Clearwater River. It was founded in 1861 in the wake of a gold rush which began in the panhandle of Idaho the previous year. Lewiston was named after Meriweather Lewis of the Lewis and Clark Expedition, which passed through the valley on their return trip of 1804-06.

The area was first visited by David Thompson in 1803, while looking for a fur trading post for the Hudson Bay Company. In 1863, Lewiston became the capital of the newly created Idaho Territory. As the gold boom quieted in the Northwest, the capital moved to Boise in 1866, an unpopular move.

Note:

The above descriptions of historic sites are excerpts taken from Wikipedia, the free Encyclopedia.

Historic Players

John "X" Beidler

Born August 14, 1831 in Mount Joy, Pennsylvania and raised at Chamsborg, Beidler had only a cursory education. He started working as a shoemaker, but found the trade did not agree with him, changed to brickmaking, and then to work as a broom-maker. He was of Dutch forebears, preferred the nickname "X" which came from his middle name, Xavier. His given height was five foot six inches, but in photos his rifle is taller than he is. He did have a short temper, but was congenial and generally liked. Disappointed in a love affair, he moved to Elkhart, Illinois, and then to Kansas to try farming, but that also gave out. He joined John Brown partisans taking part in border affrays. Brown went east to meet his destiny, and Beidler went to Texas, Colorado, and then to Virginia City in 1863. He gravitated to the Vigilantes and became famous among them. He was the principal hangman when five of Plummer's gang were hanged in Virginia City on January 14, 1864. He remained in the forefront of the Vigilante movement in the pursuit and elimination of desperadoes throughout the history of the Vigilance Committee. He later rode shotgun on several stage coaches and was appointed deputy U.S. Marshal where he was quite effective. He never made much money, but saved none of it. He had friends, and in 1889, they introduced a bill to afford him relief, but it was killed in the legislature. He died in Helena in 1890. He was a Player in Montana history as the member of the Vigilantes and self-appointed Hangman.

Thomas Josiah Dimsdale

John Buchanan, Proprietor of the *Post*, sold the paper to the firm of D. W. Tilton and Co., who hired Professor Thomas J. Dimsdale as editor. The *Post* was printed weekly in a log building with a sod roof, but was moved by Tilton into a stone addition of his book store in 1865.

Dimsdale was born in 1831 near Thirlsby, a small town in northern England into a family of engineers and public works contractors. Of small build, he called himself, "the runt of the family." He suffered pulmonary problems which limited his physical ability. He received a preliminary education in the preparatory school of Rugby. His family later desired he study for the ministry and sent him to Oxford. Financial problems of the family caused cessation of a university education in his sophomore year.

He emigrated to Ontario, Canada until the gold discovery in the Rocky Mountains, when Dimsdale decided to venture south to Virginia City. Being unable to work in the mines because of pulmonary problems, he began to teach. When the Territory of Montana was created in 1864, then Governor of the territory, Sidney Edgerton, appointed Dimsdale superintendent of public instruction of the territory. There were no duties, no schools...and no salary! Without schools in the area, people were willing to pay liberally and he succeeded. (A log schoolhouse still stands in Nevada City, Montana, where it is believed he taught.)

Dimsdale was an unbiased, quick witted, and fluent, descriptive writer. He was recognized first through his writing as the editor of the *Montana Post* and then as an author. He had ability to observe and perceptively describe the turbulent historic events of the 1860's. The actions of the Vigilante heros and the eclipse of Henry Plummer has been read by the public for over 145 years in his book "*The Vigilantes of Montana.*"

Thomas J. Dimsdale died on September 22, 1866 at age 35, leaving a widow as his only relative in the country. He was of the Protestant Episcopal faith and at his bedside during his last days was close friend, Colonel Wilbur F. Sanders. He was a member of Montana Lodge No. 2, and was buried with Masonic funeral services in the old section of Virginia City Hillside Cemetery.

Sidney Edgerton

Born in 1818 in Cazenovia, New York, Sidney Edgerton had a sickly childhood. His father went blind and died when Sidney was only six years old. His mother, a seamstress, sent him and five older siblings to family members for care.

At twenty-six years old in 1844, Sidney moved to Akron, Ohio, became interested and studied law. He earned his degree at Cincinnati Law School. In 1852, he was elected Prosecuting Attorney of Summit County, Ohio. He had an ardent commitment against slavery and showed contempt to its proponents. He was elected to Congress in 1858, reelected for a second term in 1860, and later chosen as Delegate for the Republican Party.

He declared himself an agnostic and almost reversed his upcoming marriage to Mary White. Because of his rigid beliefs, his life had been threatened and he carried a cane with a sheath that held a sword for protection.

He did not attempt to regain his nomination to Congress, lost through gerrymandering. In 1863, President Lincoln rewarded him for his service to the Republican Party, by naming him as Chief Justice to the new Idaho Territory.

To make the long trip to his new position in the Northwest portion of the country, Edgerton formed a small family group, which included his nephew, Wilbur Fisk Sanders. He was never able to take office in the Idaho Territory as Chief Justice because he could not find anyone qualified to swear him into office.

He was instrumental in lobbying Congress and talked to President Lincoln about formation of the Montana Territory. He would become Montana's first Territorial Governor in 1864, at the request of President Lincoln. (*A Decent Orderly Lynching*, Frederick Allen, pg 281; *Thrapp's Encyclopedia Of Frontier Biographies*, vol 3, pg 1262)

George Ives

He was a Player in Montana history as a member of the Plummer gang and first to be tried for Murder.

Born in Ives Grove, Wisconsin in 1836, Ives was handsome, light complexioned and nearly six feet tall. He was smooth shaven and had lively blue eyes. He left a widowed mother and several sisters to go west in mid 1850. Mining in California and in Walla Walla, Washington he became a herder of government mules. He developed a taste for rustling, making off with the animals, saying they had perished in the severe weather. He soon became a gambler and rowdy in all mining settlements of the Salmon River, showing up at Lewiston, Pierce City, Elk City, Florence and at Warrens' "diggin's." By this time he had become close friends with Aleck Carter. He was a resident of Bannack in 1862 where he met with Henry Plummer and a member of James Stuarts' Yellowstone expedition of 1863. His murderous threats and similar indiscretions are well documented *(See Chapter 13, "Shootings")*. He was likable, but when he took to drinking, his company was to be avoided. While working as a clerk and grazer for horses he learned where and when travelers would be on the trail and how much gold they carried, an important piece of information to the Plummer gang.

Ives, with Steve Marshland, held up a stage in November of 1863 between Virginia City and Bannack and on one occasion Ives held up businessman Anton Holter. He robbed and killed likable Nicholas Tiebalt of Virginia City, and was found guilty and hanged on December 21, 1863. He was the first of the Plummer gang to be arrested by James

Williams of the soon to be formed Vigilance Committee. His trial
in Nevada City by Wilbur Sanders brought Ives into the forefront of
Montana Vigilante history. (Thrapp's EOFB, vol 2, pg 710)

Nathaniel P. Langford

Nathaniel Pitt Langford, as a player, wrote and chronicled some of
Montana's intriguing history. He was a leading businessman in Bannack,
a former Banker, and as a current member of the Masons, he played a
major role in the Vigilance Committee and formation of the Montana
Vigilantes. Born in 1832 and raised in Oneida, New York, he entered
banking in St. Paul, Minnesota, in 1853. He came to Bannack in 1862,
at age 30, with the Fisk expedition, serving as third in command of
the Minnesota wagon train. He moved to Virginia City in 1863 where
he opened a sawmill. Langford became federal Collector of Internal
Revenue when Montana became a territory in 1864, and served until
1868. President Grant appointed him Governor of Montana Territory
in 1869, but the appointment lacked approval of the U. S. Senate. In
1870 Langford joined the Washburn-Doane Expedition to Yellowstone
Wonderland and was instrumental in the creation of the area into
Yellowstone National Park. He served as the Park's first Superintendent
from 1872-77. As a player in Montana history, he kept a descriptive
journal and wrote *Vigilante Days and Ways* in 1890. In 1905 he wrote
The Discovery of Yellowstone National Park. He returned to a business
in St. Paul, where he died in 1911. His book is great reading to take
readers back some 140 years to the most intriguing people and events of
Montana's beginning. (Thrapps EOFB vol-2, pg 811-12)

John S. Lott

Born on November 25, 1830 in Lottsville, Pennsylvania, he attended
trade school to learn carpentry. In 1857 John and brother Mortimer
journeyed to Marshall County, Kansas where they purchased a ranch.
In 1863 John came to Nevada City, Montana Territory, with a wagon
load of merchandise to sell to the miners. Mortimer joined him and
they purchased a store in Nevada City and operated it together for
several years. The store had the only safe in the region and many miners
deposited large amounts of gold. During their time in Nevada City,
John was actively involved in the formation of the Vigilante movement.
He composed the Vigilantes' oath of allegiance and served as a juror

during the trial of George Ives. John Lott was an active participant in the formation of the second Vigilance commitee, as well as being instrumental in securing W.F. Sanders for the Ives' trial in Nevada City. During the Territorial governorship of Sidney Edgerton, Lott was appointed Auditor for two terms. In 1865, John and Mortimer moved their store to the Twin Bridges area, northwest of Nevada City, to raise vegetables to sell to the miners. At the time there was no town site and few residents. The brothers built a pair of bridges, one over the Beaverhead River and one over the Big Hole River, giving the town its present name. John Lott died in Twin Bridges, Montana on May 24, 1910. (Montana Historical Society-Research Center)

Electa (Bryan) Plummer

Electa Bryan, 20 years old, arrived from Hancock County, Ohio in late May, 1862 on the steamship *Emile* at Fort Benton, with her sister, Martha Jane and brother-in-law, James Vail, and a former banker, Francis (Frank) Thompson. After her life in a sedate existence in Ohio, she looked forward to new adventures in the growing West. Thompson, after getting to know her on the trip, described Electa as "spirited and determined." They traveled to the Sun River, where her brother-in-law would set up and manage a government farm to teach and "civilize" the local Indians.

She met and soon married Henry Plummer on June 20, 1863, at Sun River by Father Minatre of St. Peter's Jesuit Mission, with Joseph Swift, Jr. as best man and Frank Thompson as "bridesmaid." (Electa's sister did not approve of Plummer and would not be a part of the ceremony). Electa wore a brown calico dress and Plummer wore a suit and his favorite long-coat with red lining. Swift wore moccasins, both made for the same foot. The married couple rode to Bannack in the "ambulance" of the government farm, a small covered wagon drawn by four ponies. Thompson later stated she lived in Bannack with her husband, "...in a palisaded log house with no companion of her own sex..." until her sister's family left the government farm and moved to Bannack. In September, 1863 she unexpectedly left Bannack for her home in Iowa. She later rejoined her sister's family on a farm outside Vermillion in the Dakota Territory. She remarried a widowed rancher, James Maxwell, on January 19, 1874, giving birth to two sons. She died in 1912 and was buried in Wakonda, South Dakota.

Henry Plummer (Plumer)

Henry Plummer was born in the 1830's in the Pleasant River Valley on the coast of northern Maine. Frail and poor, he suffered from chronic lung problems, living with his family in his grandfather's extended household. Genealogy records show several Henry's born into several families in the Addison township. All but two have been eliminated as being the Henry Plummer of Montana history. The most likely family is that of Moses Plumer IV, married to Abigail "Nabby" Wass. Family history was difficult to trace because Henry, unnamed at birth, was one of several "Henry's" born in the area.

Henry's actual birth date was also difficult to determine...not matching the age quoted by several writers for some of the noted events in his life. The family name was originally spelled with one "m" (Plumer), but through mistakes in the press and some public records it evolved, at least for Henry, into the more commonly used version, "Plummer." The family was laced with seamen, including Henry's father, who sailed as a steward on the ship, *Belgrade* to the California gold rush. He was found dead in his bunk at the San Francisco port in 1849. In the diary of Jared Nash, a crew member, a sickness laid waste to the ship, killing three. Moses Plumer IV, Henry's father, was apparently the fourth.

A brief summary of the "Plumer" family ancestry by Frederick Allen in his book, *A Decent, Orderly Lynching*, referencing the *Early Pleasant River Families of Washington County, Maine*, (Camden: Picton Press, 1997, pp. 462-74) led to the rejection of a statement that Henry Plumer's parents were Jeremiah and Elizabeth Handy Plumer! Jeremiah Plumer was married to Elizabeth "Betsy" Wass, not Elizabeth Handy! Jeremiah and Betsy had a son, Marion Handy Plumer, but he died in 1853. Jeremiah's brother, Moses Plumer, IV married Abigail "Nabby" Wass, (not "Elizabeth" Wass) and they had an unnamed (and unrecorded) son, born between 1830-35. By later research of historical census records (1800's) and events, he is deemed to be the Henry Plummer of the Northwest, specifically of Montana history.

At about nineteen years old in 1852, Henry felt the urge to go west and take part in the California Gold Rush. He went first to New York, then sailed to Panama, across the isthmus by mule, then by steamer to San Francisco and finally to a cheap boarding house on Bush Street. The choice of suffering hard labor in a gold field didn't appeal to the frail Plummer. He was told the chances of getting rich working a claim were virtually nil. Instead he got a job as a store clerk, devoting his spare time to the faro and monte tables in San Francisco's gaming halls. He developed skill at gambling and cards, which put him as part of a bawdy and somewhat unsavory crowd.

Early in 1853, having saved some money, Plummer took a turn at ranching. With a partner he raised cattle north of Nevada City, about 150 miles northeast of San Francisco. His enthusiasm for ranching lasted less than a year. Moving into Nevada City, a bustling mining town with the third largest population in California, he became a salesman for a local bakery. At twenty-one, he liked the hustle of urban life, the people, the saloons and the company of women. He progressed as salesman, earning enough to buy out one partner's share of the United States Bakery. He also bought a two-room bungalow on Spring Street. (The site of his former house in Nevada City is currently occupied by Telephone Co. offices).

His idea to sell the bakery and reopen at a new location proved to be a financial disaster. The economy was down and Plummer was ready to quit the West and go home, but he didn't. As luck would have it, a vacancy opened in the Sheriff's office. He became deputy, and then Marshal. The hotbed of California politics and the lure of gold, led him to seek his luck in the West and into Montana history. His killings grew giving birth to the Montana Vigilantes...and his termination in 1864.

Paris Pfouts

Paris Pfouts was born on January 9, 1829, a Player in Montana History as the President of the Vigilante Committee.

The von Pautz family came from Germany and settled in Pennsylvania. He was the fourth of ten children, apprenticed in the pressroom of the *Ohio Democrat* newspaper, moved several times in the Ohio Valley area, then traveled 4-1/2 months to Placerville, California arriving in September, 1849. He spent the winter of 1850 in the Trinity mountains, in a two room cabin without comforts. Panning the Trinity River he accumulated $600 in gold dust and spent the next four years in the gold camps. Pfouts gained experience in gold mining, playing cards...and drinking. He returned to St. Joseph, Missouri, in the spring of 1854, worked and then bought half interest in the *Gazette* as editor and publisher.

In the spring of 1855 he married and joined the Freemasons, where he soon became Worshipful Master of the Lodge. He was down on his luck, decided to head back to the west, and moving to Colorado, opened a store in Denver. He joined the local Lodge and for the second time in a year became the Lodge Master. Another business reversal made him decide to choose the Montana gold fields as his next stop. He arranged to send his family back home and send the store's supplies to Alder Gulch. Settling in Virginia City, he opened a store, a 16 by 32 foot log cabin with dirt roof, on Wallace street in November of 1863. Pfouts could easily see the injustice of gold camp law. Upon meeting Wilbur Sanders, one could hardly make any match between them, other than both sharing the idea of how to correct the injustice. Pfouts writes in his memoirs he was alarmed at the crime wave in the town and was determined to do something about it. At one of the Vigilance Committee meetings, which Pfouts did not attend, he was voted into the Presidency of the organization. In 1867 Pfouts and his family left Virginia City to return home. He never returned.

"Colonel" Wilbur Fisk Sanders

Sanders was born on May 2, 1834 in Leon, New York, where he attended the common schools and taught school in New York. He was a nephew of Sidney Edgerton (First Montana Territorial Governor). He moved to Ohio in 1854, where he continued teaching, studied law in Akron and was admitted to the bar in 1856.

During the Civil War, he served in the Union Army, under James A. Garfield, a future President. He was recruited into a company of infantry and a battery of artillery in the Union Army in the summer of 1861. He was commissioned a first lieutenant in the 64th Regiment, Ohio Infantry, of which he was made adjutant. He assisted, in 1862, in the construction of defenses along the railroads south of Nashville. When his term of enlistment expired, he resigned from the army.

He married Harriet (Hattie) Peck Fenn and had two sons, James and Willie.

Sanders arrived in Bannack in mid-September, 1863, with his Uncle, Sidney Edgerton. They had traveled by ox-driven wagon, with families and servants, from Missouri, to Salt Lake City, over the Monida Pass and into present day Montana. Their party was misdirected to Bannack in the eastern portion of the Idaho territory, rather than to the west and the newly designated capitol at Lewiston. Edgerton was to be installed at Lewiston as the presidentially appointed Chief Justice of the new Idaho Territory. (See Sidney Edgerton Portrait).

He settled in that part of Idaho Territory, which later became Montana, where he engaged in the practice of law and also became interested in mining and stock raising.

He was a young lawyer when he moved to Montana in 1863. He was there before courts were organized and, being one of the first permanent settlers, took a prominent part in bringing law and order to Montana. Sanders became prosecutor for the famous, or infamous, Montana Vigilantes who took the law into their own hands after over one hundred men had been ambushed and murdered for their gold in Bannack and Virginia City, Montana.

He acted as prosecutor in the murder trial of George Ives in Nevada City, in December of 1863, which led to the hanging of Ives and more of Henry Plummer's "road agents." It would steadfastly involve him in the Vigilance Committee and in the ultimate formation of the famous, original Montana Vigilantes.

In 1873 Sanders became a member of the Territorial Legislature and next was a United States Senator. Also, he realized the importance of preserving early records and for thirty years, as the president of the Montana Historical Society, established in 1865, he accumulated newspapers and documents in his law office.

He became known as "Colonel" Sanders. He was a Republican candidate for election in 1864, 1867, 1880 and 1886 as a Delegate to Congress and was a member of the Territorial House of Representatives of Montana from 1873 to 1879.

Upon the admission of Montana as a State into the Union, he was elected as a Republican to the U.S. Senate and served from January 1, 1890 to March 3, 1893. While in the Senate, he was chairman of the Committee on Enrolled Bills (Fifty-second Congress).

Sanders died in Helena, Montana, age 71, on July 7, 1905, and was interred in Forestvale Cemetery there. Sanders County, Montana is named in his honor.

A life size statue of Sanders adorns the Capitol in Helena, Montana.

Jack Slade

Joseph Alfred "Jack" Slade was born to Mary Kain and Charles R. Slade, Jr. on January 22, 1831, in Carlyle, Illinois. He had four siblings and would become one of the West's most feared and written about men. His father served as a U.S. Marshal, an Illinois state legislator, and was elected to Congress in 1832, but took ill and died in 1834. Jack would be raised by his stepfather who he greatly admired. Unfortunately there is little history of J. A. "Jack" Slade's earlier life and much of his later life comes from " heresay" stories.

He was deemed to have had decent schooling due to his ability to read and write and conduct business. He left home at an early age, possibly because of the death of an elderly German drifter who was reportedly struck on the head by a rock, whether intentionally or by accident, is sketchy. Apparently the incident caused Slade to leave home at only thirteen years of age to live with relatives in Texas.

Slade returned to Carlyle in 1846 and lying about his age, enrolled in the Illinois Foot Volunteers to fight in the Mexican War. His bravery was evident in the service and he was called upon repeatedly for special details. Duty as a teamster on the supply lines along the Santa Fe Trail taught him a great deal about combating Indian marauders, as well as learning the freighting business. After the war, he was discharged on October 16, 1848, as a Private, and only eighteen years old. He was described on his discharge papers as five feet six inches, dark complexion, black eyes and light hair. His education as a teamster in the Volunteers proved valuable. He later worked with several freight lines including the Overland Stage Line.

Francis McGee Thompson

He was a player in history as a storekeeper in Bannack and a boarder with Henry Plummer. Frank Thompson was an energetic traveler and entrepreneur and hoped to make good of the gold strikes in the new northwest country. He had crossed the Bitterroot Mountain Range eight times already in his brief visits.

Francis McGee Thompson was born on his grandfather's farm in 1833 at Colrain in northern Massachusetts. The family of his mother, Elvira Adams, could be traced back to Henry Adams of the 1600's. He was educated, briefly attending Williston Seminary. At twenty-two years of age, he worked in Cincinnati at Wrights Banking and Exchange office. He later took part in a political campaign at the Republican National Convention in Chicago, where Abraham Lincoln was nominated for President. He had personally met Lincoln earlier at Lincoln's Law Office in a business situation. At twenty-eight, in 1861, he decided not to join the Wisconsin Volunteers in the Civil War, but remembering Horace Greely's words, he decided to head west, to the gold country.

He entered the Idaho Territory at Fort Benton, by way of the Missouri River on the *Emile*, a passenger steamboat, with twelve other partners of the newly formed American Exploring & Mineral Co. After exploring and mining at Gold Creek the partners of the company split and each headed to other venues. Left with the mining equipment of the company to sell, Thompson saw the advantages of selling tools to miners, rather than using them himself. He opened a general store in Bannack in 1862. He had six brothers and sisters, one of which, Hugh, a mineralogist, helped him by buying and shipping supplies from St. Louis for his Bannack store.

He was a churchgoer and a choir leader in Bannack and became close friends with Sidney Edgerton, the appointed Chief Justice of the Idaho Territory, who became Montana's first Territorial Governor. He befriends Wilbur Fisk Sanders, a lawyer, and a leader of the Montana Vigilantes. He also shared a Bannack rooming house with Henry Plummer.

Thompson lobbied Congress in 1864 to create the Montana Territory, and under Governor Edgerton, gained a seat in the council as representative for Beaverhead county. About two and a half years later he returned to the states where he opened a New York office, marketing Montana mining properties. He retired to Greenfield, Massachusetts where he became Town Clerk, Lawyer, and then, Probate Judge. He married and had a daughter. He is the designer of the original "Oro Y Plata" logo for the new Montana Territory. In 1912 he wrote the book, "*A Tenderfoot in Montana*," referencing the Gold Rush, Vigilantes and the Montana Territory. This is a great reading, also giving an exclusive insight into some of the intricacies of Henry Plummer.

James "Cap" Williams

"Cap" or "Captain," as he became known as a trail master, soon became an Executive Officer of the Vigilance Committee. He was born in 1834 in Greensburg, Pennsylvania. Most of his early years are unknown. He went to Rock Island, Illinois in 1855 for two years, spent a year in Kansas where he took an active part in the 1857-58 border troubles as a Free State man. He then went to Pikes Peak, Colorado in the fall of 1858 for the gold rush. Then he piloted a wagon train into Montana, where he acquired the nickname "Captain" over a run-in with Jack Slade. He later said of Slade, " . . . I never had a man with me that I got along with better." *(See Chapter 20).*

He arrived in Alder Gulch, June 20, 1863. Williams established a corral and livery business and eventually built a ranch southwest of Nevada City. For some time he ran a pack train between Virginia City and Elk City, Idaho. He married in 1866 and raised seven children. Described as "sensitive, shy, self effacing," he was "uneducated, inarticulate, and reticent." He was a most unlikely choice to head the famed Montana Vigilantes. He was the Executive Officer of the entire activity which resulted in the execution of more than a score of desperadoes (some dispute that figure, putting it higher). He was elected Commissioner of Madison County in 1870, and unsuccessfully ran twice for the Sheriff's office. In 1865 he was a V.P. for the Montana Historical Society. His name is not mentioned in Dimsdale's book, *Vigilantes of Montana*, because Montana's Supreme Court Justice, Lew Callaway, who knew Williams in later life, said Williams and Dimsdale had a "falling-out," and Williams gave explicit orders that it should not appear.

Callaway, who had lived with Williams as a youngster for an extended period, told he had mild blue-gray eyes that turned black when angered. He was also described as strong, five foot ten inches and 190 pounds.

Williams, at first unwilling to act as the Vigilante Executive Officer, but once on the job, became a master. He was a rancher by trade, but with seven children and a wife who became strongly dissident to his activities, it became a struggle to make the ranch succeed. Acting as cosignor on a bank note for a friend, Dr. Don Byam (acting Judge in the Ives trial), who failed to pay, the creditors liquidated his ranch and sold off all the cattle. He restocked the cattle, only to loose all of them again in a deadly winter storm of 1887. Shortly afterwards the loss drove him to commit suicide. They found him lying dead in the field with an empty bottle of laudanum nearby.

James "Cap" Williams gravesite at a cemetery in Montana.

REFERENCE INFORMATION BY CHAPTER

CHAPTER 1: Henry Plummer comes to Montana
1. - A Decent, Orderly Lynching, Frederick Allen; pg 57-58
2. - Ibid; pg 17-26, pg 373-n2, (Ancestry.com\Plumer)
3. - Ibid; pg 27
4. - Ibid; pg 28-29
5. - Ibid; pg 31-37
6. - Ibid; pg 29-31

CHAPTER 2: Plummer's Ploy In San Quentin
1. - A Decent, Orderly Lynching, Frederick Allen; pg 38-46
2. - Ibid; pg 47-50
3. - State of California vs. Henry Plummer - Trial Transcripts

CHAPTER 3: Experience...True Teacher
1. - It Happened in Montana, James A. Crutchfield; pg 28-29
2. - A Decent, Orderly Lynching, Frederick Allen; pg 52-62
3. - Perilous Passage, Edwin R. Purple; pg 148

CHAPTER 4: Plummer...Homesick
1. - The Montana Frontier, 1852-1864, Granville Stuart; pg 232
2. - A Decent, Orderly Lynching, Frederick Allen; pg 69

CHAPTER 5: Cleveland...Drunken Duel
1. - A Decent, Orderly Lynching, Frederick Allen; pg 73-76
   - Perilous Passage, Edwin R. Purple; pg 137-139
2. - Vigilante Days and Ways, Nathaniel P. Langford; pg 87
3. - Ibid; pg 96
4. - Ibid; 1912 Ed; pg.184-186, 1996 Ed; pg 112-115

CHAPTER 6: Plummer...Prods Sheriff Crawford
1. - Vigilante Days and Ways, Nathaniel P. Langford; pg 106
2. - Ibid; pg 92-96
3. - Ibid; pg 97
4. - Vigilante Days and Ways, Nathaniel P. Langford; pg 98

CHAPTER 7:
Part One - Marriage & Murder
Part Two - Dillingham Murder
1. - A Decent, Orderly Lynching, Frederick Allen; pg 99-100
2. - Ibid; pg 118-119; 123-125
3. - A Tenderfoot in Montana, Francis (Frank) Thompson; pg 147-148

191

4. - Vigilante Days and Ways, Nathaniel P. Langford; pg 133-135
   - Ibid; 1912 Ed; by McClug & Co.; pg 217-218
5. - Vigilante Days and Ways, Nathaniel P. Langford; pg 133-135
   - Ibid; 1912 Ed; by McClug & Co.; pg 219
6. - Vigilante Days and Ways, Nathaniel P. Langford; pg 107

CHAPTER 8: Colonel Sanders reaches Bannack
1. - Bannack Montana: Then and Now, Robert McPherson; pg 45
2. - Biscuits and Badmen, W. F. Sanders and Robert Taylor; pg 4-20
3. - Ibid; pg 25
4. - A Tenderfoot in Montana, Francis Thompson; pg 276, n11

CHAPTER 9: Thompson meets Cutthroats
1. - A Tenderfoot in Montana, Francis M. Thompson; pg 145-147
2. - A Decent, Orderly Lynching, Frederick Allen; pg 118-121
3. - This Bloody Deed, Ladd Hamilton; pg 84-87, 206
4. - A Tenderfoot in Montana, Francis M. Thompson; pg 153-160
5. - Vigilante Days and Ways, Nathaniel P. Langford; pg 197-201

CHAPTER 10: Bummer Dan & Southmayd Robberies
1. - A Tenderfoot in Montana, Francis M. Thompson; pg 160, 276
2. - Vigilante Days and Ways, Nathaniel P. Langford; pg 139
3. - A Decent, Orderly Lynching, Frederick Allen; pg 139-140
4. - Ibid; pg 137-140
5. - Ibid; pg 155-161
6. - Vigilantes of Montana, Thomas J. Dimsdale; pg 71-77
7. - Vigilante Days & Ways, Nathaniel P. Langford; pg 150-156

CHAPTER 11: Moody Wagon Train Robbery
1. - A Decent, Orderly Lynching, Frederick Allen; pg 148
2. - Biscuits and Badmen, W. F. Sanders and Robert Taylor; pg 33-34
3. - Vigilante Days and Ways, Nathaniel P. Langford; pg 169-171
4. - Ibid; pg 172-75
5. - A Tenderfoot in Montana, Francis M. Thompson; pg 166-168
6. - Vigilante Days and Ways, Nathaniel P. Langford; pg 141

CHAPTER 12: Sanders prosecutes First Trial
1. - "X" Beidler: Vigilante, Sanders & Bertsche; pg 33-38
2. - Vigilante Days and Ways, Nathaniel P. Langford; pg 176-183.
3. - Montana's Righteous Hangmen, Lew L. Callaway; pg 25-31
4. - A Decent, Orderly Lynching, Frederick Allen; pg 3-12
5. - Vigilantes of Montana, Thomas J. Dimsdale; pg 78

6. - "X" Beidler: Vigilante, Sanders & Bertsche; pg 54
7. - Ibid, pg 57-59

CHAPTER 13: George Ives Trial
1. - A Decent, Orderly Lynching, Frederick Allen; pg 176
2. - Biscuits & Badmen, W. F. Sanders & Robert Taylor; pg 48
3. - "X" Beidler: Vigilante, Sanders & Bertsche; pg 59-61
4. - Ibid; pg 59-60
5. - Vigilantes of Montana, Thomas J. Dimsdale; pg 79
6. - Vigilante Days & Ways, Nathaniel P. Langford; pg 177-178
7. - Vigilantes of Montana, Thomas J. Dimsdale; pg 83-93
8. - A Decent, Orderly Lynching, Frederick Allen; pg 180-181
9. - "X" Beidler: Vigilante, Sanders & Bertsche; pg 66-67
10.- Vigilantes of Montana, Thomas J. Dimsdale; pg 81
11.- "X" Beidler: Vigilante, Sanders and Bertsche; pg 70-76
12.- Vigilantes of Montana, Thomas J. Dimsdale; pg 98-101
13.- Vigilante Days & Ways, Nathaniel P. Langford; pg 184-188
14.- Vigilantes of Montana, Thomas J. Dimsdale; pg 103-104
15.- Biscuits & Badmen, W. F. Sanders & Robert Taylor; pg 55

CHAPTER 14: Vigilance Committee
1. - Vigilantes of Montana, Thomas J. Dimsdale; pg 116-118
2. - Ibid; pg 116-118
3. - Montana's Righteous Hangmen, Lew Calloway; pg 41, 43

CHAPTER 15: Hang 'Em...on their History
1. - A Tenderfoot in Montana, Francis M.Thompson; pg 180-182
2. - Vigilantes of Montana, Thomas J. Dimsdale; pg 129-132
3. - Vigilante Days & Ways, Nathaniel P. Langford; pg 224-226
4. - Hanging Around the Big Sky, Tom Donovan; pg 565-576

CHAPTER 16: Virginia City Cordon
1. - A Tenderfoot in Montana, Francis M. Thompson; pg 184
2. - Vigilantes of Montana, Thomas J. Dimsdale; pg 133-135
3. - Vigilantes of Montana, Thomas J. Dimsdale; 137-138
4. - Vigilante Days and Ways, Nathaniel P. Langford; pg 233-238
5. - A Tenderfoot in Montana, Francis M. Thompson; pg 182-183
6. - Vigilantes of Montana, Thomas J. Dimsdale; 139
7. - A Decent, Orderly Lynching, Frederick Allen; pg 244-249
8. - Vigilante Days & Ways, Nathaniel P. Langsford; pg 233-242
9. - Vigilantes of Montana, Thomas J. Dimsdale; 140-149
10.- "X" Beidler: Vigilante, Sanders & Bertsche; pg 89

- A Decent, Orderly Lynching, Frederick Allen; pg 249
11.- Vigilantes of Montana, Thomas J. Dimsdale; pg 148-149
12.- Vigilante Days & Ways, Nathaniel P. Langford; pg 241-242

CHAPTER 17: Vigilantes begin Roundup
1. - Vigilantes, Hoffman Birney; pg 298
2. - A Tenderfoot in Montana, Francis M. Thompson; pg 191
3. - Vigilante Days and Ways, Nathaniel P. Langford; pg 243-249
4. - Vigilantes of Montana, Thomas J. Dimsdale; pg 150-162
5. - Ibid; pg 163-169.
6. - A Decent, Orderly Lynching, Frederick Allen; pg 259-272
7. - Vigilante Days and Ways, Nathaniel P. Langford; pg 250-254

CHAPTER 18:
Part One - Slade meets Langford
Part Two - Hero Slade: Too Big for His Boots
1. - Vigilante Days and Ways, Nathaniel P. Langford; pg 278
2. - An Ear in His Pocket: The Life of Jack Slade, Roy Paul O'Dell and Kenneth Jessen; pg 27-31
3. - Ibid; pg 53-58
   - Slade! The True Story of the Notorious Badman, Bob Scott; pg 106-117
4. - Vigilante Days and Ways, Nathaniel P. Langford; pg 283
5. - A Decent, Orderly Lynching, Frederick Allen; pg 14
6. - Slade! The True Story of the Notorious Badman, Bob Scott; pg 172-175
7. - Vigilante Days and Ways, Nathaniel P. Langford; pg 286
8. - An Ear in His Pocket: The Life of Jack Slade, Roy Paul O'Dell and Kenneth Jessen; pg 85
9. - Vigilante Days and Ways, Nathaniel P. Langford; pg 462

CHAPTER 19: Montana...What's in a Name
1. - The Bloody Bozeman: The Perilous Trail to Montana's Gold, Dorothy M. Johnson; pg 107
2. - A Decent, Orderly Lynching, Frederick Allen; pg 280-289
3. - Vigilantes of Montana, Thomas J. Dimsdale; pg 181-285
4. - Ibid; pg 187-90
5. - A Decent, Orderly Lynching, Frederick Allen; pg 298-299
6. - Ibid; pg 295-300
7. - Ibid; pg 301-03
8. - Vigilantes of Montana, Thomas J. Dimsdale; pg 192-195
9. - A Decent Orderly Lynching, Frederick Allen; pg 303-306

10.- Vigilantes of Montana, Thomas J. Dimsdale; pg 196-99
11.- A Decent, Orderly Lynching, Frederick Allen; pg 314

CHAPTER 20: Original Leaders Complain
1. - A Decent, Orderly Lynching, Frederick Allen; pg 309-310
2. - Ibid; pg 334-39
3. - A Decent, Orderly Lynching, Frederick Allen; pg 342-43
4. - Biscuits & Badmen, W. F. Sanders & Robert Taylor; pg 75

EPILOGUE: Quotes on Vigilante Justice
1. - A Decent, Orderly Lynching, Frederick Allen; pg 249
2. - Ibid; pg 249-250
3. - Ibid; pg 250
4. - Ibid; pg 254
5. - Ibid; pg 358
6. - Ibid; pg 358
7. - Vigilantes of Montana, Thomas J. Dimsdale; pg 169
8. - Vigilante Days & Ways, Nathaniel P. Langford; pg 253
9. - A Tenderfoot in Montana, Francis M. Thompson; pg 193

REFERENCE MATERIAL/BOOKS

1. A DECENT, ORDERLY LYNCHING: The Montana Vigilantes; by Frederick Allen, 1948

2. VIGILANTE DAYS AND WAYS; 1912 edition, by Nathaniel P. Langford, 1890 (Written by a Player in the Historic era.), 1996 edition

3. VIGILANTES OF MONTANA; by Professor Thomas J. Dimsdale, 1867 (Written by a Player in the Historic era.)

4. A TENDERFOOT IN MONTANA, The Vigilantes and the Birth of Montana Territory; by Francis M. Thompson, 2004 by Montana Historical Society (A Player in the Historic era.)

5. PERILOUS PASSAGE, A Narrative of the Montana Gold Rush, 1862-63: by Edwin Ruthven Purple (A Player in the Historic era.) 1995 by Montana Historical Society

6. BISCUITS AND BADMEN: The Sanders Story in Their Own Words; by W. F. Sanders II and Robert T. Taylor, (1983)

7. X. BEIDLER: VIGILANTE; Original journal notes of John Xavier Beidler; Edited by Helen Fitzgerald Sanders with William H. Bertsche, (1957)

8. MONTANA'S RIGHTEOUS HANGMEN, The Vigilantes in Action; by Judge Lew L. Callaway (A Player in the Historic era.) (1982)

9. AN EAR IN HIS POCKET: The Life of Jack Slade; by Roy Paul O'Dell and Kenneth C. Jessen, (1996)

10. SLADE! The True Story of the Notorious Badman; by Bob Scott (2004)

11. THE BLOODY BOZEMAN, The Perilous Trail to Montana's Gold: by Dorothy M. Johnson (1971)

12. THIS BLOODY DEED: The Magruder Incident; by Ladd Hamilton (1994)

13. BANNACK MONTANA, THEN AND NOW, Robert J. McPherson (2005)

14. VIGILANTES; by Hoffman Birney, 1929 Chronicle of the Plummer gang

15. THRAPPS ENCYCLOPEDIA OF FRONTIER BIOGRAPHIES; Vol. 1-3

16. COURT RECORDS: State of CA vs. Henry Plummer (Murder Trial #2)

17. VENGEANCE! The Saga of Poor Tom Cover; by Dan L. Thrapp (1988)

18. THE MONTANA FRONTIER; by Merrill G. Burlingame (1942)

19. FROM WILDERNESS TO STATEHOOD; A History of Montana 1805-1900; James McClellan Hamilton (1957)

20. THE MONTANA FRONTIER, 1852-1864 by Granville Stuart (1925)

21. THE PICK AND SHOVEL; Sons and Daughters of the Montana Pioneers Newsletter (2011)

22. FOUR FIRSTS FOR A MODEST HERO; The Grand Lodge, Ancient Free and Accepted Masons of Montana (1968)

23. HANGING AROUND THE BIG SKY; Tom Donovan, (2007)

24. BADASSES OF THE OLD WEST; Edited by Erin Turner (2010)

25. IT HAPPENED IN MONTANA; James A Crutchfield (2008)

26. BANNACK: Foundation of Montana; Rick and Susie Graetz, Montana Fish, Wildlife & Parks (2004)

27. BANNACK: Cradle of Montana; Montana Magazine; Text and Photography by F. Lee Graves (1991)

28. BANNACK: Guide by Montana Fish, Wildlife & Parks and the Bannack Association

ADDENDUM: Portraits of Places and Players

This section contains more detailed information obtained from the following sources:

Thrapps Encyclopedia of Frontier Biographies; Vols. 1-4

Wikipedia: The Free Encyclopedia

A Decent, Orderly Lynching, Frederick Allen

A Tenderfoot in Montana, Francis M. Thompson

Montana Historical Society - Research Center